D0722455

The Strangers' House

The Strangers' House

Writing Northern Ireland

Alexander Poots

TWELVE

New York Boston

Twelve
Hachette Book Group
1290 Avenue of the Americas, New York, NY 10104
twelvebooks.com
twitter.com/twelvebooks

First Edition: March 2023

Twelve is an imprint of Grand Central Publishing. The Twelve name and
logo are trademarks of Hachette Book Group, Inc.

The publisher is not responsible for websites (or their content) that are not
owned by the publisher.

Twelve books may be purchased in bulk for business, educational,
or promotional use. For information, please contact your local
bookseller or the Hachette Book Group Special Markets Department
at special.markets@hbgusa.com.

Library of Congress Cataloging-in-Publication Data
Names: Poots, Alexander, author.
Title: The strangers' house : writing Northern Ireland / Alexander Poots.
Description: First edition. | New York, NY : Twelve, 2023. | Includes
bibliographical references and index.
Identifiers: LCCN 2022047954 | ISBN 9781538701577 (hardcover) |
ISBN 9781538701584 (ebook)
Subjects: LCSH: English literature—Northern Irish authors—History
and criticism. | English literature—20th century—History and
criticism. | LCGFT: Literary criticism.
Classification: LCC PR8753 .P66 2023 | DDC 820.9/9416—dc23/eng
/20221130
LC record available at https://lccn.loc.gov/2022047954

ISBN: 9781538701577 (hardcover), 9781538701584 (ebook)

Printed in the United States of America

LSC-C

Printing 1, 2022

For my parents

Contents

At times it seems that every inch of Belfast has been written-on, erased, and written-on again: messages, curses, political imperatives, but mostly names, or nicknames—Robbo, Mackers, Scoot, Fra—sometimes litanized obsessively on every brick of a gable wall, as high as the hand will reach, and sometimes higher, these snakes and ladders cancelling each other out in their bid to be remembered. *Remember 1690. Remember 1916.* Most of all, *Remember me. I was here.*

—Ciaran Carson, *Schoolboys and the Idlers of Pompeii*

Author's Note

Northern Ireland is comprised of six counties: Antrim, Down, Armagh, Tyrone, Fermanagh, and Derry. These six counties form the greater part of the ancient province of Ulster. Ulster's three remaining counties—Monaghan, Cavan, and Donegal—are part of the Republic of Ireland. The partition of Ireland, on 3 May 1921, divided not only the island, but Ulster as well.

Nationalists view Northern Ireland as a colonial hangover, and often favour alternative expressions for the region. 'The North of Ireland' is the most common of these in print, though 'The Six Counties' (along with variations like 'the Upper Six' or 'the Occupied Six') is used frequently enough in conversation, in song lyrics, and on social media to be noteworthy. In the Republic, most people refer simply to 'the North'.

For Unionists, Northern Ireland is an integral part of the United Kingdom. It is the name of their country and their home. Unionists waxing poetic may sometimes refer to Northern Ireland as 'Ulster', although this is not as common as it used to be.

A word on religion. It is true that the vast majority of Nationalists are Catholic, and that an overwhelming number of Unionists are Protestant. Consequently, religious affiliation has often been used by journalists as a shorthand for political belief. This has given rise to the view—in England, at least, astonishingly widespread—that the Troubles were in essence a theological dispute that spilled out of the divinity schools and into the streets.

The reality is quite different. Religion may be a useful shorthand, but it is a shorthand that records only a fraction of what is said. Certainly faith has played a vital part in shaping Northern Irish society. This has always been a conservative part of the world, though things are changing, at least in urban areas. Decades of scandal have lamed the Catholic Church. Sinn Féin, the largest force in Nationalist politics, is avowedly socialist in orientation. And although Presbyterian and Evangelical denominations remain powerful in

Unionist political circles, their influence on broader society is much reduced, at least among the young. The internet is a great leveller.

These are recent developments. Yet even fifty years ago, when the Catholic Church still held sway and Presbyterian ministers still spit fire from the pulpit, religion was rarely the primary source of friction between communities. Access to good land and decent employment, combined with competing ideas of what and where home is, are of much greater importance to the history of conflict in Northern Ireland.

I am aware of how much like a vocabulary list this note appears. Reality has never been so simple. The real story of Northern Ireland exists in the gaps between the blanket terms and the binary opposites. This is something which the men and women who write well about this place have always understood.

Alexander Poots, Belfast, January 2022

Introduction

Ireland is water country leased to solid ground. When the end comes, it will come in a long seep, the rivers pooling out to meet as friends, loughs unnamed by sea. Final lights on the hilltops: Donard, Mullagh-cleevaun, Carrauntoohil. Then the fussing of damp firewood—last of the human smells—and a lifting at the waist as land drops away, lease expired.

Water is a great temptation for the Irish writer. James Joyce opens *Ulysses* atop a Martello tower overlooking Dublin Bay, where Buck Mulligan muses on 'The snotgreen sea. The scrotumtightening sea.' The first word of *Finnegan's Wake* is 'riverrun'. Standing on a grey pavement, W. B. Yeats is recalled to 'The Lake Isle of Innisfree' by the sound of 'lake water lapping' within his heart. There is no escaping the water. Eavan Boland's 'Cityscape' (hardly a promising title for the literary dowser) is a poem about light, but takes in a trip to the seawater baths, finds Dublin forever 'unsettled between sluice gates and the Irish Sea,' and closes with the image of a glass eel, 'a translucent visitor / yearning for the estuary.' Jonathan Swift wrote his first great work, *A Tale of a Tub*, while a clergyman at Kilroot, a small place on the northern shore of Belfast Lough. Irish literature is suffused with a chill damp that lingers between the toes. The sea, as Buck Mulligan observes, is 'our great sweet mother.'

Every Irish city sits beside a trembling flatness. Belfast, Cork, and Derry have their sea loughs. Dublin crouches low to the bay. Galway braves the North Atlantic. Limerick is almost a delta city, straddling the Shannon as it finds the ocean. Waterford's name tells its own story. Out in the countryside are the peat bogs, the streams, the brown water standing at the edge of fields. The punkish algae advancing always across bus stops and machinery and the windows of half-built homes. Moss grouting walls. The hills are green and indigo, except for a few days in the winter cold, when they pale into white. Water is a constant companion on this island, the writer's natural reference and resource.

I begin with water because Northern Ireland is

liquid in every possible sense. Books about this place are usually prefaced by a glossary of political positions and cultural identities. I have succumbed to this temptation myself in order to give a basic orientation to readers unfamiliar with Northern Ireland's unique vocabulary, but such thumbnail sketches are always failures in the end, bungalows built on floodplains. They are failures because they attempt to order a watery world, in which liquids become solid for a time, only to melt away again.

This acceptance of a liquid world unites the writers in this book. Many would be suspicious of a work which claims to be about 'Northern Irish' writers, and rightly so. A common birthplace is no guarantee of common purpose, especially a birthplace that many would regard as illegitimate. It would be foolish to pretend that writers share anything of significance just because they are from the same place. Northern Ireland is a political fact, but the same cannot be said for its culture. Michael Longley, frustrated with the attempts of journalists and scholars to corral the poets who emerged in Belfast in the 1960s and '70s into a literary movement, said: 'I don't think for a split second we thought in terms of Northern Irish poetry or Ulster poetry or being Ulster poets... There was no group, there was no school, there was no manifesto.' Are not writers like Seamus Heaney, Derek Mahon, Medbh McGuckian, and Louis Mac-Neice simply *Irish*, without qualification? Indeed, to follow Longley's argument to its natural conclusion, are they not simply *poets*? Each of them wrestled with these questions in their own way, but the novelists and poets in this book do share a deep awareness of change, uncertainty, and even threat. Above all, there is homesickness.

When David Trimble and John Hume accepted the Nobel Peace Prize in 1998, Trimble chose to speak of Northern Ireland as a house: 'Ulster Unionists, fearful of being isolated on the island, built a solid house, but it was a cold house for Catholics. And northern Nationalists, although they had a roof over their heads, seemed to us as if they meant to burn the house down.' This is more than a useful metaphor. The long and desperate story of the British colonisation of Ireland—a story that predates the Northern Irish state by at least three hundred years—has seen writer after writer grasp for an elusive home. Inevitably they fail, and that failure becomes the subject of their work.

Tom Paulin's poem 'An Ulster Unionist Walks the Streets of London' is about a man who expects to feel at home in the capital of the United Kingdom.

Instead, he discovers that he is a foreigner. The Britishness he believes to be his birthright is withheld—not aggressively, but in the accumulation of small things. In the (southern) Irish enclave of Kentish Town, he feels only "a half-foreigner"—an upsetting realisation. There is kinship with the Irish, whether he wants it or not:

> *What does it feel like?*
> *I wanted to ask them—*
> *What does it feel like*
> *to be a child of that nation?*

That nation. The question he cannot ask, of course, is slightly different: "What does it feel like to be a child of *a* nation? Of *any* nation?" Here is the ultimate fear of the Unionist, that home is not where it was always supposed to be. The key does not fit the lock, and no one answers the bell.

Paulin's 'Ulster Unionist' rhymes sadly with John Betjeman's 'Cockney Amorist': 'Oh when my love, my darling / You've left me here alone / I'll walk the streets of London / Which once seemed all our own.' The Cockney Amorist is bereft in his own way, finding London bombed out by his lover's absence, but it remains his city. Even in his grief, he is part of it.

The Ulster Unionist cannot say the same. Betjeman's amorist tours the music halls, parks, and tea shops in which he loved and was loved. Paulin's Unionist ends up at the Strangers' House:

> *But I went underground*
> *to the Strangers' House—*
>
> *We vouch, they swore,*
> *We deem, they cried,*
> *Till I said, 'Out . . .*
> *I may go out that door*
> *And walk the streets*
> *Searching my own people.'*

What is the Strangers' House? This is perhaps a reference to the Strangers' Home, or, to give the place its full title, the Strangers' Home for Asiatics, Africans, and South Sea Islanders. For the eighty years between 1857 and 1937, this institution provided temporary lodging for a small number of the many foreign sailors who had served on British ships, only to find themselves adrift in London at the end of their careers. The Strangers' Home was built on West India Dock Road in Limehouse, a Thameside district which was then at the centre of London's maritime commerce. Residents would stay at the Home until they could find working passage back to their own countries, most of which were subject to British imperial rule. Used up by navy and trading company, they waited at the heart of empire for a ship home. It is here that Paulin's Unionist has his final, awful revelation. This is a truth so shocking that it is only ever implied. The Ulster Unionist recognises these dispersed and exhausted subjects of the Empire. The Strangers' House, with all its watery associations, is home. He flies out into the street, 'searching my own people', but of course he has already found them. This is not a truth that he can admit to himself, and so he walks on through the London streets. All that remains is homesickness.

Tom Paulin lays bare the uncertainty at the heart of Ulster Unionism—the terrible suspicion that they are mired between Catholic Ireland and indifferent Britain, foreigners everywhere. Naturally this longing for a home is not unique to the Unionist tradition; it pervades the writing that has emerged from Northern Ireland over the past century. Writers from Catholic backgrounds have felt just as excluded and uncertain, though in a different fashion. When Seamus Heaney was asked about identity, he would answer with great care, although I suspect that he

found the invitation to parcel himself off in this way
rather crude. Such questions seem childish when set
against Heaney's work, and it is in the work that we
find an answer:

> *Once we presumed to found ourselves for good*
> *Between its blue hills and those sandless shores*
> *Where we spent our desperate night in prayer*
>   *and vigil,*
>
> *Once we had gathered driftwood, made a hearth*
> *And hung our cauldron in its firmament,*
> *The island broke beneath us like a wave.*
>
> *The land sustaining us seemed to hold firm*
> *Only when we embraced it* in extremis.
> *All I believe that happened there was vision.*
>   —'The Disappearing Island'

'To found ourselves for good'—to build a home—
is a presumption. Heaney suggests that *home*, that
solid word, among the most concrete and wholesome
in the English language, is a fantasy. The poem peels
certainties away. Only in extremis—at the point of
death—does solidity return. But not even this is sure:
the island has already broken 'like a wave', and it will

do so again. Waves are rarely solitary, after all; they build and break in succession. They will go on breaking and reforming, dousing the hearth and overturning the cauldron. At the last, Heaney holes the poem beneath the waterline: this is not what happened, it is what is *believed* to have happened. The vision is suspect. Heaney described the poem as one of a sequence chronicling his loss of faith in Irish patriotism as the Troubles drew on. Heaney's islander, like Paulin's Unionist, finds certainty washed away. Nationalist and Unionist alike find themselves adrift. They are all inhabitants of the disappearing island, tenants of the Strangers' House.

The Strangers'
House

CHAPTER ONE

A product of long corridors

Little Lea is a strange house. This strangeness is not obvious at first glance. The house has a well-fed look. It exudes the paunchy, serene air of an accountant three years from retirement. Brick walls, a mellow sanguine that comes only with time. There are generous bay windows and tall chimney stacks, perhaps a little too tall, as if some long-dead architect made a mistake with the blueprints. A large garden surrounds the house, grass giving way to mounded shrubs and, near the driveway, a young monkey puzzle. The road beyond is green in the summer, green with rhododendron, laurel, and broad trees.

C. S. Lewis did not like Little Lea. More than that, he found it strange.

Perhaps it is not a very Belfast house. No, it is not what you might expect. When I visit on a May afternoon it makes me think of southern England. Those parts of Berkshire or Surrey that are too spacious to be suburban and too pruned to be rural. I think of a woman in a chair beyond the bay window, and dust on framed photographs, and a clock ticking. It is exactly the sort of drowsy settlement described by Louis MacNeice at the start of *Autumn Journal* (1939): 'Close and slow, summer is ending in Hampshire, / Ebbing away down ramps of shaven lawn where close- / clipped yew / Insulates the lives of retired generals and admirals / And the spyglasses hung in the hall and the prayer- / books ready in the pew'. Little Lea is not the Belfast lived in by most people. And though it is neat and trim, there is a sadness to the place.

Clive Staples Lewis was born in Belfast in 1898. The first seven years of his life were spent in a semi-detached Victorian house on Dundela Avenue, in the east of the city. That house has been replaced by a block of flats, but examples of its type remain on the street, pairs of high-ceilinged villas which seem to be in a constant state of renovation. Lewis was content there, apart from the nightmares.

Nightmares. It is easy to make too much of them. All children have bad dreams. Most adults have them too, although we learn to blink them off when morning comes. Yet I am struck by the fact that the first three writers in this book—C. S. Lewis, Forrest Reid, and Louis MacNeice—all had nightmares so memorable that they seemed worthy of record decades after their occurrence. All three men described their childhood nightmares in their respective memoirs. MacNeice's sound the most unpleasant because they are not attached to anything in particular; at least Lewis had the advantage of being able to name his fears: 'My bad dreams were of two kinds, those about spectres and those about insects. The second were, beyond comparison, the worse; to this day I would rather meet a ghost than a tarantula.' Lewis managed to overcome his phobia of insects, but the ghosts were another matter.

In 1905, the Lewis family moved to Little Lea. The 'New House', as Lewis called it, is a twenty-minute walk from Dundela Avenue, and today the two places are part of the same comfortable suburban spread which marks the northeastern edge of Belfast. This was not always so. Clive's father, Albert, built the house on a site that, although close to his business in town, was at a remove from the pollution and noise of a city famous for linen mills and shipbuilding. Although the house retains its tranquil air, much has changed in the surrounding area. As a child, Lewis was able to stand at the front door of Little Lea and find nothing but fields between him and Belfast Lough. Now that same view would be obstructed by hundreds of houses, a stretch of motorway, and the concrete oblong of Belfast City Airport. The difference is most apparent at night. Today's orange wash of streetlamps and bedroom windows would seem strange to a boy used to the dark of an empty strand, broken only by the lights of ships heading to their berths.

We can guess at what Lewis might have thought of these changes. While he was more at home with prose than poetry—indeed, his enduring dislike of Louis MacNeice has been attributed to professional jealousy on that score—Lewis did write verse, and in 'Pan's Purge' (1947) he bemoaned the triumph of modernity:

> *I dreamt that all the planning of peremptory*
> *   humanity*
> *Had crushed Nature finally beneath the foot*
> *   of Man;*
> *Birth-control and merriment, Earth completely*
> *   sterilized,*
> *Bungalow and fun-fair, had fulfilled our Plan . . .*

The poem concludes with Pan's return. The goaty god tears down the cities and reseeds the earth. Man is freed from his own creation. Unplanned Pan has yet to make a reappearance in Belfast. Bungalows there are many, and although nature has not been entirely crushed, Lewis's childhood landscape is all but gone. Nevertheless, some things survive. St. Mark's Church remains the tallest structure in this part of Belfast. Lewis was christened there, and his maternal grandfather served as its first rector. The Victorian pillar of the bell tower is so large that the main body of the church seems a squat and embarrassed afterthought. This scale is appropriate, as St. Mark's had to compete for attention with the gantries and cranes of the Harland & Wolff shipyard, which still dominates the lough's southern shore. The yolk-yellow cranes that loom over Belfast today were not built in Lewis's lifetime, but their predecessors were just as vast, a forest of steel smoking at the water's edge. Harland & Wolff built some of the finest ships in the world, and on visits home from school between 1909 and 1911, Lewis would have been able to sit on his front porch and watch the hull of RMS *Titanic* grow skyward.

Things were never quite right at Little Lea. Albert Lewis had commissioned a home fit for a successful

lawyer, and to all appearances the tradesmen had
delivered. But appearances are not everything in a
house. Little Lea was draughty. The drains did not
drain and the chimneys did not draw. The place felt
too large for a family of four, even with the addition
of the cook and maids then essential in a middle-class
household. Dundela Avenue had been a home. Little
Lea was just a big house. Writing in 1955, a full fifty
years after his family settled there, Lewis described
the uncanny qualities of the new house as crucial to
his development:

> The New House is almost a major character
> in my story. I am a product of long corridors,
> empty sunlit rooms, upstair indoor silences,
> attics explored in solitude, distant noises of
> gurgling cisterns and pipes, and the noise of
> wind under tiles.

Lewis spent hours in the attics of Little Lea. When
his brother was home from school, they would play
together, but Clive was alone much of the time, a
little boy listening to the wind. He devoured books
and stories. His nursemaid had told him Irish legends
when he was very young, tales like that of Cú Chu-
lainn, the Hound of Ulster, who stood alone against

mighty armies. Now he could read for himself, and once he had started, he did not stop for the rest of his life. Mythology fascinated him, whether it was Greek, Irish, or Norse. He loved the romance of the Middle Ages, and for a while, Arthur Conan Doyle's *Sir Nigel* was his favourite novel.

It was only a matter of time before he started telling stories of his own. Animal-Land was born in the attics of Little Lea. This was the first of the fantastic worlds he created, a dream country which combined his interest in both animals and medieval knighthood. He wrote stories about the events that took place there and illustrated them himself. In his autobiography, Lewis makes much of his need to give that world an internal coherence. Animal-Land required much more than a cast of 'chivalrous mice.' The nascent scholar in him would not settle for a childish fantasia of the woolly kind. These stories mattered a great deal to Lewis. They had to make sense precisely because he cared so much for them. So he set about constructing a chronology and a geography for this strange new country. Maps were drawn and technological advances explained. He even aped the sceptical analysis typical of the historian: 'The chivalric adventures which filled my stories were in it alluded to very lightly and the reader was warned that they might be "only legends".'

Perhaps Lewis was a natural sceptic. This would be borne out by his later career, both as an Oxford don and as a Christian apologist. Much of his working life was spent probing the work of his undergraduates—sitting opposite them, listening to their weekly essays, and then slowly pulling their arguments apart over the course of an hour. Naturally, his books on the Christian faith required a different kind of scepticism. This was not the scientific, critical judgement of the scholar. It was the willingness to take stock of an increasingly secular, liberated society and dare to find it wanting. The obvious was not necessarily true. Total faith in the material world and its rhythms could leave a man open to reversals of the most sudden and devastating kind. This was a lesson that Lewis learned at Little Lea.

In early 1908, Flora Lewis disappeared. She was still in the house, but Clive was not allowed to see her. Doors opened and closed. Strangers came and went. An atmosphere of whispering in hallways and distracted adults. The sense that the life of the house was running down, failing. Abdominal cancer was diagnosed. The operation to save Flora did not take place in hospital, but at Little Lea. Clive was told nothing. After a brief reprieve, Flora died, just eight months after her diagnosis. The house, initially a large and slightly uncanny playground, had become something quite different. It was now a house of whispers, a house in which gowned figures holding trays of steel implements made familiar rooms sinister, a house in which his mother had died.

Flora's death marked the end of Clive's boyhood. Albert packed him off to school in England, recalled him to Belfast for a year, and then sent him back to England for a spell at Malvern College. Private tuition to prepare him for the Oxford entrance exams followed. He secured a scholarship to University College Oxford in 1917, and arrived to begin his studies in the April of that year, only to be called up by the British Army a few weeks later. He was a serving officer on the Western Front by November 1917. After the war he returned to Oxford and never left again.

The brief, prewar period in Oxford was a revelation. Lewis fell in love with the city, with his set of panelled rooms and the warren of quadrangles and winding lanes that cocooned them. It is difficult to imagine a more seductive place for a young man of his aesthetic bent and ferocious reading habits, and his infatuation with one of the most beautiful cities in Europe was to be expected. Rather less expected, perhaps, was the chance to meet other Irish people there. Oxford was his first opportunity to befriend Irishmen who did not hail from the bourgeois Unionist milieu in which he had grown up. Then as now, some of the most passionate Irish Nationalists were to be found living happily in England, and Lewis quickly became close to one such man in his college, Theobald Butler.

Butler's initial attraction seems to have been his impressive book collection and deep literary knowledge (he introduced Clive to many new authors, including the Marquis de Sade), but he had a political impact on the young Lewis too. Among Butler's books were the poems of Joseph Plunkett, who had been executed in May 1916 for his participation in the Easter Rising. When they tired of Nationalist literature, Lewis and Butler spent many contented hours discussing the innumerable and egregious failings of the English people. Writing home to a friend in Belfast, Lewis described a typical conversation with Butler: 'Like all Irish people who meet in England we ended by criticisms on the invincible flippancy and dullness of the Anglo-Saxon race. After all, there is no doubt, ami, that the Irish are the only people: with all their faults I would not gladly live or die among other folk.' By the summer of 1917, Lewis had come to reject what he clearly regarded as the

rather vulgar Unionist politics of his upbringing in
favour of the romantic overtures of 'the real Ireland':

> 'Tis true that I have no patriotic feeling for
> anything in England, except Oxford for which
> I would live and die. But as to Ireland you
> know that none loves the hills of Down (or
> of Donegal) better than I: and indeed, partly
> from interest in Yeats and Celtic mythology,
> partly from a natural repulsion to noisy drum-
> beating, bullying Orange-men and partly
> from association with Butler, I begin to have
> a very warm feeling for Ireland in general.
> I mean the real Ireland of Patsy Macan etc,
> not so much our protestant north. Indeed, if I
> ever get interested in politics, I shall probably
> be a nationalist.

'The real Ireland of Patsy Macan'. Perhaps it was
inevitable that the young Lewis believed that 'real
Ireland' could be found in a fictional character. Patsy
Mac Cann (Lewis misspelled the name) was not a politician or a revolutionary, but the central character in
a novel. *The Demi-Gods* (1914) was written by James
Stephens, one of many Dubliners who specialised
in idealised depictions of rural Ireland in the early

twentieth century. Stephens is best known today for his novel *The Crock of Gold* (1912) and for his eyewitness account of the Easter Rising, *The Insurrection in Dublin* (1916). In *The Demi-Gods*, Patsy wanders Ireland with his daughter Mary and a fractious donkey. They are joined by three angels, with whom Patsy and Mary enjoy a series of picaresque adventures. Although it was natural for Lewis to be drawn to a book with a fantastical dimension, the details of the plot matter less than the atmosphere of the novel and the characterisation of Patsy Mac Cann himself. Mac Cann's Ireland is a dream and it follows a dream logic. The impossible is commonplace there, the extraordinary swiftly assimilated: 'The Mac Canns, so far as they professed a religion, were Catholics. Deeper than that they were Irish folk. From their cradles, if ever they had cradles other than a mother's breast and shoulder, they had supped on wonder.' Stephens's gushing fable might make a modern reader squirm, but his work is not without humour, and it gave Lewis a different way of seeing his homeland.

Lewis grew up with a particular shade of Protestantism. The Protestants of Ireland have never been a single, monolithic entity. Lewis's family were Church of Ireland, the preferred faith of the professional middle classes. The more radical, nonconforming

Protestant congregations that flourished in Belfast would have been as alien to Lewis as a weekend break in a Trappist monastery. This multitude of Protestantisms is still alive and well today. A short walk from St. Mark's, the stately Victorian edifice in which Lewis was baptised, lies the Ballyhackamore Gospel Hall, a low grey building that is home to an assembly of Christian Brethren, an evangelical denomination which favours extreme simplicity of worship. Outside the Gospel Hall is a sign reminding passersby that THE WAGES OF SIN IS DEATH. A Church of Ireland man, though agreeing with the message in principle, would probably find the mode of delivery a touch de trop. Men like Lewis were raised to favour a restrained and moderate Christianity. The Church of Ireland was stately, solid, august. It was the church of the lawyer, the tea merchant, the mill owner, the doctor, and the engineer. Above all, it was the church at the heart of middle-class Unionism.

Lewis does not dwell on politics in his autobiography, yet it is clear that Unionism was part of the warp and weft of his childhood. His brother, Warren, recalled the endless political jawing between Albert Lewis and his friends during the long evenings at Little Lea: 'The religious, political and social cleavage between the Protestant Unionist and the Roman

Catholic Nationalist was as deep and rigid as that which separates the Moslem from the Hindu...No man came to my father's house who did not hold exactly the same political views as he did himself; from which it followed that there was nothing which could be properly described as discussion between host and guest at all'. Instead there was the stale rehashing of points agreed upon by everyone in the room. Talk for the sake of mutual reassurance. It is no wonder that a fey and imaginative boy like Clive found nothing to excite him in his father's Unionism. The Ireland of Belfast's upper middle class held no interest for him. The mundane urban life of 'our protestant north' was no good. For Lewis, the only reality that mattered was the romantic fantasy of Patsy Mac Cann. Many people would find such a position perverse; typically, Lewis had no difficulty in finding a novel more real than the world around him.

Lewis largely experienced the partition of Ireland through letters. His upbringing gave him some cachet with fellow undergraduates, who assumed that his trips home must have been a 'great adventure.' Many of these undergraduates would, like Lewis, have been serving in the trenches of France and Belgium just three years before, and one imagines that they were rather difficult to impress. While it was not the Western Front, Belfast had seen a great deal of violence since the Government of Ireland Act was passed in 1920. This was the legislation that created a Northern Irish state which would remain integral to the United Kingdom, while recognising an independent Irish nation. The commencement of this act, on 3 May 1921, saw the partition of the island of Ireland. Westminster politicians hoped that the act would satisfy the demands of both communities. The Irish people would finally be free to govern themselves, while northern Protestants like Albert Lewis—who feared financial ruin, political impotence, and cultural irrelevance in a new Ireland—would find their lives reassuringly unchanged.

The Government of Ireland Act 1920 was a compromise, and naturally it pleased no one. Two-thirds of the people living in the newly minted Northern Ireland were Protestant, but that still left nearly half a million Catholics marooned on the wrong side of the new border—a border that many held to be the illegitimate imposition of a foreign power. Meanwhile, Protestants remained anxious about their place in the Union. Although the establishment of Northern Ireland gave them a measure of security, they were now citizens of a tiny statelet that was dependent on the goodwill of Britain for its continued survival.

The period between 1920 and 1922 was a bloody one. Sectarian violence erupted across the North. Belfast was particularly tense, and Lewis was alarmed to discover that a police post had been erected on the street outside Little Lea: 'Your news of a post at our back gate was, I must admit, rather a shock to the imagination when I first read it. I hope it will not "draw the enemy's fire".' The comfortable enclave of well-to-do Protestants in which he had grown up was now an appealing target. Little Lea was on a war footing:

> I keep on hearing of 'battle, murder and sudden death' in the streets of Belfast. How long is this to continue I wonder? To me peace is so obviously the good and the condition of all other goods that perhaps I do not sufficiently appreciate the motives of those, in any party, who wish to settle everything by shooting. I hope you are keeping well, and that you already wear your shrapnel helmet when travelling on a tram.

It seems that the modish Nationalism of Lewis's undergraduate years was discarded as easily as his Unionist upbringing. As a grown man he despaired of both communities, and in 1950 he would describe Northern Ireland as a case study in 'the daemonic character of popular political "causes".' This is not to say that he lost faith in his real Ireland. Even once he had secured a permanent position at Oxford, he still mused about whether he should return for good: 'Certainly the actual country appeals to me more every time I go home... I find more and more a something in every Irish scene which you can't get elsewhere, and which, though not better in itself, is better *for us*. I think "roughness without severity" is the nearest one can get to it. It is grand and desolate and yet somehow one feels at home.'

That he never did go home permanently is beside the point. Perhaps everyone needs some theoretical escape, a half-planned existence running parallel to the dailyness of living, an existence with which we might one day intersect. Although Lewis remained in Oxford, he returned to Belfast frequently. He escaped for long walks in the Antrim hills whenever he could and enjoyed trips south of the border, which he referred to laughingly as the 'Iron Curtain'. Ireland was a reservoir from which he drew water for the rest of his life, and this influence can be found in his most famous creation.

Not many people would associate Narnia with

Ireland. On the contrary, a casual reader of the books will come away with an almost overwhelming impression of Englishness. Think of the names of those children, the ones who leave our world through a wardrobe. They are the safest, most English names imaginable: Peter, Susan, Edmund, Lucy. The children themselves are essentially interchangeable. The only one of them that really sticks in the mind—no doubt because he has a mind himself—is Edmund, the boy who succumbs to temptation in *The Lion, the Witch and the Wardrobe* (1950). Edmund alone fails to live up to the vision of the perfect English schoolboy. The rest of them act like bank managers in training. They are forever telling each other to stop being silly or to go to bed, and are always ready to offer a miniature homily, whether it has been asked for or not. When reading the Narnia books, I think of the first chapter of William Golding's *Lord of the Flies*, when the children on the desert island are full of sensible ideas and grand plans that the reader knows will degenerate into chaos and bloodshed within fifty pages. But in Narnia, of course, the chaos never comes; winter ends, the prince is rescued, threatened order is always restored. In *Lord of the Flies*, the naval officer who rescues the children looks at the feral survivors and muses sadly that 'I should have thought that a pack of British boys—you're all British aren't you?—would have been able to put up a better show than that'. The children of Narnia would meet his expectations all right.

This is not a criticism of Lewis. It is simply to observe that Narnia embodies a particular idea of How Children Should Behave that flourished in English literature in the years following the Second World War. Arthur Ransome, Enid Blyton. They were all at it. The purse-lipped moral rectitude of these rather blank, earnest characters is a quintessentially English fantasy of childhood. The settings, too, contribute to the Englishness of the series. The children in *The Lion, the Witch and the Wardrobe* have been evacuated from a bombed-out London. *The Silver Chair* opens in the depressing environs of an experimental school. The postwar malaise of 1950s Britain is a constant background hum—Edmund's acceptance of the Turkish delight offered to him by the White Witch makes much more sense when you consider that sugar was rationed in England until 1953. It is difficult to imagine that any trace of Lewis's Ireland could be found in such English books. But such a trace is there. You just have to look for it.

Decades in Oxford did not diminish Lewis's love for rural Ireland, and his letters to friends and family

in Belfast are full of reminiscences about the walks
he had taken along the coast and across the ridges.
Lewis always judged the English countryside against
his aesthetic benchmark, the landscapes of Ireland's
north. The soft fields and little rivers of Oxfordshire, while lovely, were deemed 'not exciting', and
Cornwall seemed an imitation of Antrim and Down
rather than a place with a genuinely unique character. As a student, Lewis had dreamed of placing his
favourite city within his beloved Irish landscape: 'I
often think how lovely 'twould be if you could take
up this city of Oxford bodily and put it down somewhere "*By a northern sea*", between the mountains of
Donegal.' The Narnia books allowed Lewis to do just
that. Take this description of Narnia's capital, Cair
Paravel:

> The castle of Cair Paravel on its little hill
> towered up above them; before them were the
> sands, with rocks and little pools of salt water,
> and seaweed, and the smell of the sea and long
> miles of bluish-green waves breaking for ever
> and ever on the beach.

This passage from *The Lion, the Witch and the Wardrobe* faithfully reproduces the Irish coast—Donegal

would fit, but so too would the shores of Down—
and Cair Paravel, with its towers, halls, and shining
windows, is a fantastic Oxford lifted bodily from
England and given new surroundings, a translation
worthy of a saint. When Susan and Lucy fly across
Narnia on Aslan's back, their view is one familiar
to anyone who has walked in the Glens of Antrim
or the Mourne Mountains: 'roaring waterfalls and
mossy rocks and echoing caverns, up windy slopes
alight with gorse bushes, and across the shoulders
of heathery mountains and along giddy ridges and
down, down, down again into wild valleys'.

The Mournes were at the heart of it all: 'I have
seen landscapes, notably in the Mourne Mountains
and southwards, which under a particular light made
me feel that at any moment a giant might raise his
head over the next ridge.' Today the Mournes are a
popular hiking destination. You are more likely to
encounter a flying column of teenagers uniformed
in the latest sportswear than a giant. But they remain
an extraordinary place, and a strange one too. As one
drives south through County Down, they bubble
up from the green plain without warning. There is
none of the gentle preparation that topography usually affords a range of hills, no slow swelling of the
earth to meet them. The Mournes appear suddenly

and grow in the windscreen until they mass into a wall on the horizon. They are not true mountains, yet somehow they deserve the title. Their suddenness creates this mountainous effect. In a fey mood, I could well believe that they were an intrusion from another world. A granite protuberance forcing its way through to us as the result of some metaphysical fluke.

If you approach the Mournes from Newcastle, your climb begins next to a stream. Water plates and twists on the rock, white when it moves and black when it pools, gathering for the next run. The stream runs between broad trees and an understory of rhododendrons and ferns. The rhododendrons are, I suppose, escapees from Victorian gardens. Their ancestors were rooted on the slopes of the Himalayas, but these rhododendrons are here, on the last outpost of a faraway continent, happy in Irish earth. The work begins beyond the tree line, where the yellow gorse—whin, as it is known here—takes over from the trees. The ground steepens as the path winds towards a saddle between two blunt, brown hilltops. Donard to the left, Commedagh to the right.

Up on the ridgeline, the hills roll out and away towards the sea. The ground is boggy in the hollows, and the grass there takes on luminous colours. In the right light, the ground could be dusted with saffron, while at other times it is a rude and livid green. There is sea to the east and Carlingford Lough to the south, and for great stretches there is room for only a tiny road between the hills and the shore. Lewis loved that contrast, the way the granite brows simply stop and the eye playing over ridgelines must suddenly widen to take in the water, water that in the evening becomes indistinguishable from sky. A town called Rostrevor sits on the lough shore, Mournes peering over the rooftops, and it was here that Lewis found his other world, the final fulfilment of Animal-Land: 'That part of Rostrevor which overlooks Carlingford Lough is my idea of Narnia.'

Narnia was not made from landscape alone. Lewis drew freely from his Belfast childhood, and there are many local myths surrounding the sources of his inspiration: the lion-headed door knocker on the St. Mark's rectory that suggested Aslan, for example, or the black Victorian lampposts that still stand on Crescent Gardens. Whatever the truth of these claims, the continued influence of Little Lea is certain. He was a product of the long corridors of that strange house, after all, and perhaps he never really found his way out of them.

The most direct use Lewis made of his upbringing

was in *The Magician's Nephew* (1955). Chronologically, this is the first in the series, and serves as Narnia's book of Genesis. Aslan breathes life into a blank void, creating animals, plants, mountains, and streams. He grants some creatures the ability to speak. He also comes face-to-face with the malign principle that will haunt Narnia forever: Jadis, Queen of Charn, an embodiment of evil who appears time and again in various baleful incarnations throughout the series.

The book opens with Digory, a boy who must stay with his unpleasant uncle. Both of Digory's parents are absent in their own way. His mother is dying, while his father is away in India. Parents have no place in Narnia. Of course, parents are one of the great problems of children's literature. They tend to get in the way of the story. A child cannot go wandering off on an adventure if he is expected home for supper, and so his mother and father must be dispatched by the end of the first page. The angry rhinoceros must eat James's parents before he can find his Giant Peach. Huckleberry Finn is the son of a selfish drunk. Harry Potter is an orphan, and Lyra Belacqua grows up as one. The kids are on their own. They have to be if anything interesting is going to happen to them. But the Chronicles of Narnia take this necessity to an extreme. Harry Potter mourns his parents; the children of Narnia rarely even mention theirs. The schoolchildren who populate the series are found in the homes of distant and uncaring relations, or on train platforms, or crying behind the school gym block. They are without homes.

The parallels with Lewis's own life are particularly acute. Digory's mother, dying in a house that is not her home, is the most obvious, and the saddest, of the resonances. But the house itself is the true ghost. Digory meets a girl called Polly, and the new friends quickly realise that they are able to gain access to each other's house without having to bother with doors. The way in which their houses are connected is, of course, through the attic:

> It is wonderful how much exploring you can do with a stump of candle in a big house, or in a row of houses. Polly had discovered long ago that if you opened a certain little door in the box-room attic of her house you would find the cistern and a dark place behind it which you could get into by a little careful climbing. The dark place was like a long tunnel with a brick wall on one side and sloping roof on the other. In the roof there were little chinks of light between the slates.

Polly has created her own little world in the attic, a 'smuggler's cave' filled up with empty bottles that once contained ginger beer. The attic is also the means by which the children happen upon the private study of Digory's uncle. This uncle, a man best described as unscrupulous, is a magician who has discovered a method of travelling between worlds. Too cowardly to attempt the journey himself, he tricks Polly and Digory into taking the plunge.

Lewis created a new world in the attics of Little Lea. As a grown man, he was able to fulfil the wish he had held since childhood, that a purer realm would break through into our tawdry reality. Digory and Polly do not have to create a different, magical world as they fumble about in their dark attic spaces. They find that such a world—indeed, such *worlds*—do not need to be fabricated or imagined. They need to be discovered.

In *The Lion, the Witch and the Wardrobe*, Peter, Susan, Edmund, and Lucy have been chased out of London by German bombs. They are sent to an old house in the countryside to stay with an elderly Professor. The reader knows that this Professor is none other than Digory, now an old man. Lucy has discovered Narnia through the wardrobe and tells her siblings about her adventures there. The other children ask the Professor what he thinks of Lucy's yarn. They are shocked by his reply. He does not dismiss Lucy as a liar. He does not call her a fantasist or an attention-seeker.

The Professor simply says: 'I should warn you that this is a very strange house, and even I know very little about it.'

*　*　*

Lewis left Little Lea. He left Ireland, and while he was away, his birthplace acquired a new name. Northern Ireland was a place he visited often, a place where he took his wife for their honeymoon, but he never lived there. Yet his childhood stayed with him. Perhaps he lived in that. He wrote to his father frequently, long and detailed letters, and this was not the only person in Belfast with whom he corresponded.

Lewis met Arthur Greeves when they were both young. They bonded over a shared love of Norse mythology and remained close until Lewis's death in 1963. It was the most important and enduring friendship of Lewis's life. While Clive went to school in England and built a life for himself in Oxford, Arthur stayed in Belfast. The two men exchanged letters for decades, swapping news, discussing books, planning the walks they would take when Lewis was next in Northern Ireland. As young men they discussed sexual fantasies, and as they grew older, they indulged in one of the great pleasures of middle age: moaning about what they saw as an increasingly bleak and depressing world. Lewis sent him advice too. In one letter written in 1930, Lewis set out a long and considered analysis of what it means to be a writer. This was a no-nonsense and rather unsympathetic response to Greeves's admission that, although he wished to write, he was muted by his fear of failure. Lewis had suffered in a similar fashion, and offered a simple remedy: 'I think the only thing for you to do is absolutely to *kill* the part of you that wants success.'

This was a friendship that permitted discussion of every type. Nothing was forbidden, and the advice on offer was not always of a purely literary character. When still a teenager, Greeves had confessed to an appreciation of male beauty that was, to put it mildly, unusual in a scion of the Belfast bourgeoisie. Lewis was happy to talk this over with Greeves, though what he described as 'your particular taste' was not shared by him. He was satisfied that Arthur's interests were rooted in a yearning for abstract beauty. Still, Lewis worried about his friend, especially when Greeves began to spend more and more time with Forrest Reid, a Belfast novelist who specialised in fiction of a mythological and often sensual nature. In 1931, Lewis sent Greeves some more advice:

> Be careful of Reid. I am sure he is in danger of stopping at the purely sensuous side of the Greek stories and of encouraging you to do the same.

CHAPTER TWO

Be careful of Reid

I n 1905, a young man from Belfast published a slim novel called *The Garden God: A Tale of Two Boys*. The author wrote of one youth posing another on the seashore, first as a faun, then as *Spinario*, then as Dionysus, garlanded with seaweed. He wrote of kisses in the night: 'Just then, when his lips had touched Harold's cheek, he had given himself to him for better or worse, had given him his life, his trust.' He wrote of 'the messenger of Eros; the fair boy who had come to him from his strange garden, his meadow of asphodel.' He wrote all this just ten years after Oscar Wilde had been sentenced to two years' hard labour for gross indecency.

Forrest Reid was the youngest of twelve children,

one of only six to survive. The family lived in reduced circumstances. Reid's father was a Belfast man who had moved to Liverpool and done well in the shipping business. At the height of his career, he owned his own merchant vessel, which he sent across the Atlantic during the American Civil War. Reid was unclear about the details, but it seems that his father had hoped to slip his vessel through the Union blockade and had sunk everything into the venture. The ship was captured, and the Reids found themselves in financial difficulty. They left Liverpool and returned to Belfast, making a home at 20 Mount Charles, a broad street of rouged stone terraces in the south of the city. This is where Reid was born in 1875.

Both the Irish and the English take enormous enjoyment in tearing down beautiful buildings. The people in charge of such things clearly feel that too much architectural beauty poses a danger to public morals. Although Belfast has not suffered quite so badly as Dublin, much is gone forever. Carefully pointed brickwork and elegantly proportioned streets have been replaced by plastic cladding and plate glass. Large tracts of the city center are now so banal that they are effectively invisible. But Mount Charles has survived. It is a time-stained place these days. Empty rooms wait behind the bay windows. A

scrubby public garden at one end of the street is covered with discarded syringes, and buddleia has com-
mandeered the guttering. Though it is at the heart
of the university quarter, an area busy with students
and drinkers, the street has a backwater feel.

Young Forrest went out every day in his sailor
suit and straw boater. Emma, his nanny, took him to
the Botanic Gardens. His favorite place was the glass-
house, where he would wander between the ferns and
palms, enjoying the good rich smell of damp earth.
While inside, he would press his nose against the glass
and look at the gardens beyond: 'What I saw there,
in spite of the familiar shape and position of each
tree and shrub, was not the Botanic Gardens at all,
but a tropical landscape, luxuriant and gorgeous...
Tigers and panthers burned in those shrubberies, and
scarlet, green, and blue parrots screamed soundlessly
in the trees.' He often felt on the brink of *breaking
through* and entering that paradise, but the moment
never came. He wanted to escape. In later life, he
came to believe that all art was an escape attempt,
though one doomed to fail. Reid was homesick for a
place he had never visited. 'Divine homesickness,' he
called it, 'that same longing for an Eden from which
each one of us is exiled.'

Darkness brought the nightmares. He slept alone

in a little room at the top of the tall house. One night
Emma woke him. Reid recalled kneeling on his bed
in his nightshirt with his arms around her neck. She
was dressed for a journey. She left his room and went
downstairs and never returned. Her loss was devastating. Emma had been a constant presence in his
life; she had walked with him, talked to him, read
to him. Now she was gone, and the night became a
stage upon which weird actors played. The dark was
'like a vast rotting body swarming with obscene life.
I could hear stealthy movements; I dared not open
my eyes, because I knew hideous things were there,
waiting, gloating, eager to display before me their
half shapeless horror.'

Matters cannot have been helped by a change of
address. Reid's father had died, and the family now
moved across the street to 15 Mount Charles. The
new house was cheaper, smaller, and on the side of
the street that received no direct sunlight. Number
15 had a sinister aspect from the beginning. The gas
jets were turned down low to save money, and so the
house dozed in constant gloom. One of the bedrooms
was haunted. The housemaid said that she had seen
a man on the bed, his jaw bound up like a corpse's,
but his cold eyes alive and staring. The wardrobe was
even worse. C. S. Lewis would write of a wardrobe

as a gateway to a magical new land, but Reid saw only a sarcophagus: 'How often had I seen its doors open stealthily (and oh! so slowly), while the pale waxy fingers of a dead hand just appeared between them.' Ghosts were everywhere. His departed nanny, his dead father, the six siblings he would never know. Reid had pressed his nose against a pane of glass and seen a better world. Now another, darker realm was trying to push its way through to him. The nightmares went on for years.

Nightmares terrify because they are experienced as real. It was Reid's good fortune to discover another form of sleeping reality. For him, it was not true dreaming at all, but a form of return. An exile while awake, he found home again in his dreams. He called this place 'a kind of garden' and 'a remote Atlantis.' The dark of his bedroom was replaced with an arcadian landscape. Cool, mossy glades sloped down to the sea. The sun always shone, and animals of every kind basked and played. The ghouls and fetches that had once massed at the edge of his vision were banished. In their place came someone who was to define Reid's life and work:

And presently, out from the leafy shadow he bounded into the sunlight. I saw him standing for a moment, his naked body the colour of pale amber against the dark background—a boy of about my own age, with eager parted lips and bright eyes. But he was more beautiful than anything else in the whole world, or in my imagination.

Reid's dream companion is described with an obvious erotic charge. This is the first thing a reader notices. But it is important to look beyond the parted lips. Reid was a lonely boy. *Apostate*, his autobiography, mentions several boyhood friendships, but none of them were of any depth. He did not attend school until 1888, when he was already a teenager, and had only his much older sisters at home for company after Emma's departure. The Adonis that Reid dreamed up on Mount Charles was first and foremost an answer to that loneliness, to the unwelcome isolation that seems to have persisted for his whole life. Reid's novels all centre on what he called 'the friendship theme.' This can be taken as little more than a coy reference to same-sex love. As we will see, there is no doubt that Reid loved young men, perhaps to the point of obsession. But this was more than eroticism glossed in Hellenism. The friendship theme must be taken at face value. And that theme is not salacious, but deeply sad. True connection always eludes the hero. Time and again in Reid's novels, the reaching hand meets nothing but empty air.

Reid went to school at the Royal Belfast Academical Institution—mercifully shortened to 'Inst' by locals—but formal education passed over him without ruffling a hair on his head. He took a job in a tea warehouse, and it was there he began to write. Later he went to Christ's College, Cambridge. He seems to have enjoyed his time in England, but he hurried back to Belfast the moment he had taken his degree. He could not picture a life beyond Ireland. And he could not imagine a life in which he did not write. So he settled down in Belfast and began.

Reid disowned his earliest attempts at writing, declaring that he 'had every fault except insincerity.' *The Garden God* (1905) was his second book. It is a slim work, more short story than novel. Graham Iddesleigh enjoys the same dream life as his creator. He too visits Arcadia, he too has an ideal companion. When he goes to school, he meets Harold Brocklehurst, the very image of his dream boy. The two youths fall in love. Their affair is not explicitly sexual, but nor is it innocent. Reid does not attempt to hide the narrative thrust. Graham and Harold are well aware that they have embarked on something which must remain a secret: 'Hush! Speak lower. If you were caught here with me, you know, there'd be the most frightful row.'

Harold spends the summer holidays at Graham's house in the country. They take a boat out and wonder if the sea around Ireland is haunted. When they stop in an inlet, Graham invites Harold to pose for him. Graham proceeds to direct his companion in a queer *tableau vivant*. Graham's gaze turns Harold, naked on the wet rock, into *Spinario*, and then into a young god: 'You are too young for an athlete. Your body is too slender. I will make you into a youthful Dionysius instead. Let me put this seaweed in your hair. It is a wreath of vine.' The chapter culminates with the pair making a pagan offering to the spirit of the place, which they identify as the Unknown God. They pray for 'that thing which may be best for him.' Harold is killed by a runaway horse on the next page.

The mature Reid wished to consign *The Garden God* 'to the darkest corner for disowned juvenilia,' and with good reason. The prose is overgrown, the plot choppy, the pacing a disaster. Harold's end is so abrupt that, to paraphrase Oscar Wilde, one must have a heart of stone to read the death of Harold Brocklehurst without laughing. Yet the novel is still of great interest. All of Reid is here, and the themes that he would develop and refine for the rest of his life are fully present, albeit in a rather crude form. The perfect friendship. A pagan delight in the natural world. The beauty and power of youth.

This obsession with youth, that fatal trap, had a morbid weight. Harold dies immediately after the boys have prayed for 'whatever is best.' For Reid—the Reid of 1905, at any rate—it was obvious that aging was a fate worse than death. This was more than an aesthetic pose. At the age of sixteen, Reid had been so distraught at the thought of approaching adulthood that he had attempted to kill himself with an overdose of laudanum. Laudanum, the poet's peace. The attempt was a failure, but it left him bedridden for days, somewhere between life and death. Later, Reid would describe twilight as having 'an opiate beauty.'

Youth was the theme to which he returned again and again over the next forty years of writing. And although the subject matter of his books did not change, his writing did. The prose became controlled and clear, and the plots unfurled gently, though always animated by their own strange logic. These books—which number at least seventeen novels, two autobiographies, and studies of W. B. Yeats and Walter de la Mare—never made their author a household name, but he did win the respect of his peers. His greatest champion was E. M. Forster, who became a close friend after meeting Reid on a visit to Belfast in 1912.

Forster admired Reid. He liked his self-sufficiency and he loved many of his books. He was interested in the 'friendship theme' too. And perhaps he was in awe of a man who dared to write as Reid did. Although Reid's mature writing never equalled the transparent eroticism of *The Garden God*, young male bodies lounge on every page. Youth, both as a physical fact and as a symbol of a lost Eden, is hunted, desired, celebrated, and lost. Reid was exasperated by writers who were dishonest about their real subject matter. The most striking example of this came early in his career.

As a debut novelist, Reid had begun to exchange letters with Henry James, who offered him writing advice and book recommendations. Reid, emboldened by his correspondence with the great man, wrote to ask whether he might dedicate *The Garden God* to him. James accepted, only to react with horror when he received his complimentary copy. A tart letter was sent to Belfast, and Reid found himself suddenly out of favour:

And the Master was not pleased . . . it was clear that [*The Garden God*] had produced in him an intense exasperation—all the greater because he would not come out into the open and let me have the cause of his annoyance plump and plain. Strange that this slender tale, removed from actuality and placed in an eternal summer, should have been regarded as a dangerous and subversive work.

No one who has read *The Garden God* would think it necessary for James to state his objections 'plump and plain.' James had spent a lifetime weaving his own desires into subtle, suggestive novels. *The Garden God* was anything but subtle and left very little to suggestion. For a man like James to be associated with it had all the makings of a scandal. Reid was unrepentant. In his second volume of autobiography, *Private Road* (1940), he scorned James's 'strange moral timidity, which refuses to accept responsibility for what deliberately has been suggested.' The question, of course, isn't why Henry James exhibited such timidity. It is why Forrest Reid did not.

Today we are fond of classification. We subdivide ourselves into genus and species. But it was not always so. We do not know how Reid thought of himself, especially since he lived in an age rather less rich in labels than our own. Stephen Gilbert, who knew Reid for nineteen years, described him as a homosexual. But, as Gilbert himself acknowledged, Reid was repulsed by the thought of sexual contact: 'Of actual homosexual goings-on he thoroughly disapproved. So at least he expressed himself to me.'

When E. M. Forster finished *Maurice*, a novel about a homosexual relationship which would be published only after his death, he worried about sending Reid the manuscript: 'I have written a novel which cannot be published... You would, in some way, sympathise with it, but I know that in other ways it might put a severe strain on our friendship.' Forster feared that his presentation of homosexual love as something real, rather than as a component of an arcadian fantasy, would upset his friend. Reid did not do realism. There was no room for his ideal companion in the real world. Only in his summer land, his Greek dreamscape, could the love he sought be found. Anything else was crass, even repugnant. This attitude to love, sex, and literature can be difficult to understand. His friends certainly found Reid a mystery at times. As Forster wrote to him: 'I have heard you feel things I cannot, and draw distinctions that mean nothing to me.'

Homosexual relationships as they are understood today—or as E. M. Forster understood them

yesterday—were of no interest to Reid. Nevertheless, he cultivated intense friendships with young
men throughout his life. The first of these flourished
when he was still a young man himself. He was
working at Musgraves, the tea warehouse. A new lad
called Andrew Rutherford arrived as an apprentice.
Reid took him down to the docks on a cold morning
to show him that side of the business. And as they
walked along the wharf, through the chaos of crates
and shouting dockers, Reid began to fall in love with
the shy young man beside him. Their lives became
entwined. They worked together in the day and
discussed books and music by night. Reid made no
attempt to disguise the romance of that time: 'Sometimes, indeed, the sunshine, filled with little dancing
golden dust specks, touching his hair or his cheek,
would set me dreaming of him as a kind of angel who
had strayed into this world by chance'. Rutherford
was not only Reid's first love. He was his first audience too. In *Apostate*, Reid described showing Rutherford his private journal. This act of exposure took
place in one of the attic rooms at 15 Mount Charles.
He recalled the way Rutherford's dark hair fell across
his brow as he read. The slight flush on his cheek.
The gentle lamplight, the silent house. Seduction à
la Reid.

It did not last. It could not. Andrew Rutherford betrayed Reid in the worst possible way—he grew up. Other young men arrived over the years, but the same problems arose. They married, or moved away, or died. Reid's dreamland, a world in which youth set like amber, would have to be written about rather than lived. This became more true with every passing year. Rutherford was Reid's contemporary; his later amours were not. Time's gulf opened and would not close. Still, if Reid could not hope for the perfect friendship he had dreamed of as a child, he continued to invest a great deal in young men. They fed his writing. Not poetic waifs, but cheerful, embodied youths. There was simple pleasure to be found in the very fact of them. And he enjoyed styling himself as teacher and mentor.

Stephen Gilbert was his last obsession. Gilbert, an aspiring writer, learned much from Reid. Yet he looked back on their friendship with ambivalence: 'During all the nineteen years I knew him my feelings for Forrest Reid were mixed. Time and again I wished he would take himself out of my life, that he had never come into it. I felt bitterly that he had stolen my youth.' Reading Gilbert's words, I think of *The Garden God*, and Graham posing Harold on the rocks. Perhaps Reid could not see his young men as individuals with lives of their own to lead. They were beautiful things to be posed. To be arranged *just so*. Characters in a novel.

Reid attempted to pose Stephen Gilbert in *Brian Westby* (1934). Martin Linton is a novelist in late middle age. The world has dried up on him. He cannot write. His doctor recommends a period of total rest. So he goes to Ballycastle, a resort town on the north coast of County Antrim. On the beach he spies a fair-haired boy. At this point the reader begins to anticipate a reworking of Thomas Mann: *Death in Ulster*, Gustav von Aschenbach convalescing by the Irish Sea. But this is not quite how things turn out. Linton notices that the boy, Brian, is reading one of his own novels. They fall into conversation, and the two become closer and closer as the holiday progresses. Brian is the perfect eighteen-year-old. He is masculine yet boyish, intelligent but not intellectual. Above all, he embodies the natural world:

> He was very untidy and very attractive, with his flaxen ruffled hair breaking into loose curls over his forehead, and his fair skin...He gave Linton the impression of being a part of his surroundings—of the sun-bleached sand dunes, the deserted shore, the blue tumbling

waves, the open sky. He gave the impression
of being more *in* nature than anyone he had
ever before met. He looked as if the cleanness
of the sea wind was in his blood; he looked as
if something of the impersonal beauty of sea
and sky and shore had passed into him and
become human.

Brian is a fledgling novelist. Linton gives him
writing advice, and they begin to work on a story
together. Then comes a twist that would make
Mickey Spillane blush. In what is surely the most
preposterous moment in Irish literature, it transpires
that Brian is in fact Linton's son, the result of a marriage that withered years before. Brian Westby is
really Brian Linton. That Linton should happen upon
a boy reading one of his own books on a deserted
beach is unlikely; that the boy should be his long-lost
son is ludicrous. Linton, eager to get to know his son
on his own terms, does not tell Brian the truth at
first. When he does, Brian must make a choice. He
wishes to stay in contact with his father, but knows
that his mother will never allow it. Does he remain
with his mother, a narrowly religious woman who
views his literary aspirations with suspicion, or go to
live with the humane and loving Linton?

John McGahern found *Brian Westby* repugnant. For him, the plot was nothing more than an excuse for an older man to pursue a youth: 'Winter coyly hiding its desire for Spring's young body beneath the cloak of Instruction.' McGahern, a remarkable writer and perceptive critic, missed the mark in this case. If Reid had wished to write a simple tale of masked desire, he would have done so. There would be no need for *Brian Westby*'s contorted narrative and outlandish coincidences. While the novel does dwell on Brian's beauty, its true subject is Linton's loneliness, and the redemption offered to him by the prospect of fatherhood. The ideal friend changes from companion to son. Andrew Rutherford is replaced by Stephen Gilbert.

The eccentric progress of *Brian Westby* might have something to do with the manner in which it was written. Reid wanted to write about Gilbert and asked the young man for his permission to do so. Gilbert, embarrassed and perhaps feeling rather objectified, agreed on the condition that he have the power of veto over the book. This is no way to write a novel, and it seems possible that the back-and-forth between writer and subject produced the book in an attempt at compromise. Gilbert was not content to pose on the rocks.

Reid was aware that his plot was ridiculous. He even joked about it in the text. Linton, musing on the improbable turn his holiday has taken and analysing his own feelings towards the situation, thinks that 'this was not the psychology that he would have put into a novel had he been treating the subject'. And at one point early in the novel, Linton criticises a 'psychological impossibility' in one of his own books. This implausible theme is deployed 'for the sake of the story' and is never successfully resolved: 'You can see the author knew this himself by the immense pains he takes to try to make it plausible. That's rather feeble, don't you think? In fact it's worse than feeble, it's insincere; and I hate insincerity. I hate it in life; and in art, of course, it's fatal.'

John McGahern argued that the themes of fatherhood and literary mentorship in *Brian Westby* were nothing but 'Jamesian lamps playing on the dark central object.' Such a connection would have horrified Reid. His plots may have been silly, but the writing itself was never anything but sincere. There was no dark central object. Unlike Henry James, Forrest Reid wrote everything 'plump and plain.' The relationship between Linton and Brian should be read just as Reid wrote it, not as an erotic cypher to be decoded behind closed doors.

McGahern's critique might have dismayed Reid, but it would not have surprised him. He was used to being an object of suspicion. The frankness of his novels gave many readers pause. C. S. Lewis's warning to Arthur Greeves about his friendship with Reid was prompted by such suspicion. Suspicion that Reid had imported the most unsavory aspects of the ancient Greeks into the modern novel. This sensuous appreciation of youth and pagan celebration of nature would be seductive to someone like Greeves, a young man interested in writing and painting who was in need of artistic guidance. Lewis wanted to keep his friend on the straight and narrow. Reid must have been aware of his reputation among Belfast's more literary types. In *Brian Westby*, Linton's marriage fails because of the publication of his novel *Hippolutos*. The novel is only ever alluded to, but the glimpses we have of its subject matter make it plain that it is a classic Reid production, an argument for ancient Greek ideals and a pagan relationship to nature.

When Lewis looked at the Northern Irish landscape, he saw a magical world. When Reid looked at the same mountains tumbling down to the sea, he saw the playground of the young gods he worshipped.

Linton's initial attraction to Brian is a form of nature writing. As we saw above, Brian is a product of the wind, the sea, the sky. Like C. S. Lewis, Reid was passionate about the Irish landscape. Unlike Lewis, Reid was able to roam in it whenever he pleased. All of his novels and stories are firmly embedded in place. His best writing is about the land, and the land was how he made sense of the boys who fascinated him. Reid's most sensual passages take place outside: 'The rain had thickened gradually and was mingled with a fog which floated in from the sea. The salt air left a moist clinging stickiness on Brian's hands and face and clothes. He could taste it on his lips, and its smell was everywhere, like the smell of wet seaweed.'

Reid's commitment to Ireland was absolute. It never occurred to him to go anywhere else. This was unusual for a man like Reid. A move to a larger city, to London or Paris or Dublin, would have been natural for a writer. Equally, given his commitment to the 'friendship theme' and love of Ancient Greece, a Mediterranean life might have suited him well. Other queer authors of his generation escaped to the more morally forgiving climes of southern Europe. Norman Douglas made a home on Capri, W. Somerset Maugham settled on the French Riviera. It is not difficult to imagine another life for Forrest Reid, to picture him sitting outside a café on the shores of Chios, smoking a pipe and watching the sun drop into the Aegean.

Yet foreign shores never tempted him away. Belfast Lough was all he required. In 1952, E. M. Forster went to Belfast to unveil a memorial plaque to Reid. In his address, he said: 'All that he valued was learnt here...he wanted to write his own sort of books in his own way and to be in Northern Ireland to do it.' Still, Forster was clearly amused by the contrast between Reid's love of the countryside and the industrial city in which he spent his life. In a piece about Reid written in 1919, Forster offered a less-than-flattering depiction of Belfast:

> One slides up to it at dawn through mists and past the clangour of shipyards. Unreal yet squalid, its streets lack either picturesqueness or plan...A clammy ooze clings to the pavements, to the dark red bricks, the air is full of the rawness though not of the freshness of the sea, and the numerous Protestant places of worship stand sentinel over huddled slums and over dour little residences whose staircases are covered with linoleum.

Forster did not want to denigrate Belfast. His point was that this little city, with its shipyards and dour houses, had produced a remarkable writer, one who would one day receive the praise that he deserved. Although that day has yet to come, Reid did gain some recognition in his lifetime. His novel *Young Tom* was awarded the James Tait Black Memorial Prize in 1944. His readership was small, but other authors recognised the quality of his prose. Even John McGahern admired his writing. Despite his distaste for the subject matter, he acknowledged the simple beauty that Reid captured in the closing pages of *Brian Westby*. Abandoned by Brian, Linton is left alone on the Irish shore: 'He found the place where they had sat that morning making their plans. But the tide was farther out now: there was a broad strip of uncovered yellow sand between the rocks and the sea.'

* * *

What were they up to, C. S. Lewis and Forrest Reid? They had so much in common. Both were Protestants of the upper middle class. Both took comfort and inspiration from the landscape of Northern Ireland. Both dreamed in the attics of tall houses as children, and both lost their anchors early on: Lewis his mother, Reid his beloved Emma. Their imaginations fed nightmares first, novels later. Neither was political, beyond a belief in peace as the highest good. Like

Lewis, Reid showed little interest in the partition of Ireland, but then he showed little interest in any of the events that occurred in the wider world—during air raids in the Second World War, he would open all his windows and blast opera from his gramophone to drown out the warning sirens. Despite their different moral visions, they were friends, of a kind, and would go on long walks through the countryside with Arthur Greeves. Perhaps it was inevitable that these two men's novels would, at times, chime with each other.

Reid regarded *Uncle Stephen* (1931) as his finest work. Forster called it a masterpiece. After the death of his father, Tom Barber goes to stay with his uncle, a reclusive old man. Other members of the family gossip about this mysterious figure. He disappeared for years in his youth, they say, and there was a scandal involving 'some very queer friends.' Uncle Stephen lives in a large manor house in the Irish countryside, surrounded by trees and parkland. He is famous in the local area for his penetrating eyes, and he dresses all in black. Tom muses that his uncle would 'have made a lovely magician.' As the story progresses, it becomes clear that he is capable of remarkable things. Tom spends his days wandering through the overgrown gardens and lazy countryside, and gradually a weirdness overtakes him, and the usual laws of space and time begin to slip away.

Forster described Reid's books as haunted, but to read *The Magician's Nephew* immediately after *Uncle Stephen* is to discover one book haunting another. Digory must also move to a new house to stay with his uncle, and he also realises that his uncle has magical abilities. He is changed by what happens next, just as Tom Barber is changed. There is no evidence that Lewis was directly influenced by *Uncle Stephen*, but the similarities are striking. Two boys, two strange houses, two magical uncles, two fantastical new worlds. The difference lies in where these books go next. Lewis's strange house was merely a starting point. Reid's was a place to stay in bliss, forever.

These days, C. S. Lewis has been effectively claimed by the English, although Belfast City Council has been putting up a decent rearguard action of late—a visitor to East Belfast can now walk around C. S. Lewis Square, where sculptures of Mr Tumnus and the White Witch peer out of the shrubbery. Yet Forrest Reid has not been claimed by anyone. This is partly because of his subject matter. As Forster wrote of his novels: 'All the characters have, or are thinking of, youth, and all the scenery is, or is trying to be, some twilit spot in the north of Ireland.' Lewis wrote universal tales, Reid wrote Irish ones. But this is not the whole story. Perhaps no one has claimed Reid because he did not write what a Protestant novelist was expected to write.

At its worst, Northern Ireland offers up an unceasing parade of casual assumptions. One of the most widespread of these assumptions is that Protestants have no authentic cultural heritage. In some cases this is a belief born of genuine ignorance; in others it is a useful angle of attack. Protestants, the argument goes, cannot make anything of their own. Land, music, poetry: everything they have must first be taken from someone else. This criticism makes sense only, of course, if there really is no Protestant culture to be found. And so the most visible manifestations of the working-class Protestant tradition—the marching bands, the sashes and banners, the great bonfires lit at midnight on the Twelfth of July—are dismissed as empty and vulgar. Equally, novels and poems written by Protestants are treated as Anglo-Saxon imports. These critiques are not confined to the less collegial fringes of Irish Nationalism. They can be found coming from within the Protestant community itself. As the historian Connal Parr noted: 'It is striking how convinced many Ulster Protestants are of their inveterate conservatism and innate lack of lyricism.'

Part of the problem is that no one seems quite sure what a Protestant literature might look like. The unspoken assumption is that a Protestant literature would necessarily be a political literature. But this is a fatally narrow view to take. There is more to writing than the advancement of a cause or the promulgation of a manifesto. Literature is not propaganda. The best novels offer something much more than that. The clean surfaces and straight lines of political causes are not found in them. Good novels are sticky and untidy rooms in strange houses. They admit to the messiness of life.

In *Private Road* (1940) Forrest Reid wrote:

Although Irish, I had never been interested in politics... had never distinguished in my mind north from south, and the Ulster propaganda did not particularly appeal to me. It was not what would today be called Ulster propaganda, since it was definitely nationalist, and merely insisted that Ulster should play its part in the Irish Revival. I had no objection to that naturally, but I could not see why there should be two camps.

It is difficult to imagine a writer less interested in politics. Naturally, his lack of engagement was itself a position, and a very middle-class Protestant position to boot—he had the luxury of not caring what the politicians were up to. Furthermore, Reid's books fit none of the stereotypes associated with Ulster Protestantism: they are queer, allusive, beautiful, and fantastical.

And yet, despite everything, he was a Northern Irish Protestant novelist, and his books reflect his culture and his class. Here is a Protestant literature, ready and waiting to be claimed. It is not what most people might expect, but it exists nonetheless. He loved his country, everything about it. His dreamland was a summer evening in Ulster, and his youths were always Irish youths: 'The boy looked at him and then down at the book with a quick raising and lowering of his eyebrows. The trick was unconscious, and unexpectedly at variance with his accent and manner, which pointed unmistakably to an English public school. But English boys rarely have this mobility of feature, and Linton decided that probably he was Irish.'

Probably he was Irish. For a queer fellow like Forrest Reid, there could be no greater compliment.

CHAPTER THREE

Grey Crow &
the lawyer

When still a boy, Forrest Reid saw Oscar Wilde in Belfast:

I beheld my first celebrity. Not that I knew him to be celebrated, but I could see for myself his appearance was remarkable. I had been taught that it was rude to stare, but on this occasion, though I was with my mother, I could not help staring, and even feeling I was intended to do so. He was, my mother told me, a Mr. Oscar Wilde.

Reid presents his boyhood sighting of the famous writer as little more than a curious anecdote. He was twenty years old in 1895, the year of the Wilde Affair. In early April of that year, the newspapers were full of Wilde's lawsuit against the Marquess of Queensberry. Just a few weeks later, the papers were full of Wilde's fall from grace. He became a byword for infamy in England and Ireland. Worst of all, his very name became a slur.

Reid lived through it all. The man he had seen promenading through Belfast was now circling a prison yard. How did they make him feel, those broadsheets at the breakfast table? Perhaps they frightened him. An unwelcome premonition of his own future. Desire reduced to commerce, letters sent and regretted, a life spent waiting for the blackmailer's note or the policeman's knock. And yet even then Reid must have known that his life, queer fellow though he was, would not take that shape. Wilde's passions were shallower than Reid's, and much more dangerous.

The taint associated with Wilde's name outlived him by decades. Seventeen years after Wilde's death, C. S. Lewis told Arthur Greeves that he was happy to discuss male beauty, as long as they avoided 'everything that tends to sordidness (and beastly police court sort of scandal out of grim real life, like the O. Wilde story).' It was Wilde's tragedy that his carefully curated persona should come to be synonymous with 'grim real life'. Even E. M. Forster kept him at arm's length. In *Maurice*, the eponymous character confesses to his doctor that he is 'an unspeakable of the Oscar Wilde sort.'

Fifty-four years after Wilde's death, Brian O'Nolan, a Tyrone man fond of pseudonyms, who wrote novels as Flann O'Brien and a weekly column for the *Irish Times* as Myles na Gopaleen, railed against a proposed memorial in Dublin: 'Oscar Wilde was not an Irishman, except by statistical accident of birthplace. He had become completely déraciné and living in England before he was twenty. Not one shred of his literary work even suggests an Irish inflection'. Oscar's shame could not be allowed to reflect on Ireland.

Wilde's connection to the North of Ireland is little known. The fact that Wilde was Irish at all is news to some people. Born in Dublin in 1854, Wilde spent his earliest years at 21 Westland Row and 1 Merrion Square. After seven years of boarding school in County Fermanagh, he returned to Dublin for a degree at Trinity College. He did not leave for England until he was twenty years old—still young, but then he would be dead at the age of forty-six. Nearly half of his short life was lived in Ireland. And yet Oscar's Irishness can still surprise. In 1998, Jerusha McCormack, then a lecturer at University College Dublin, noted her 'frustration at having to explain to Irish students that Oscar Wilde was, yes, indeed, Irish.'

Wilde at his apogee—that brief period between the initial publication of *The Picture of Dorian Gray* in 1890 and his conviction for gross indecency in 1895—was synonymous with London theatre, London society, and London fashion. His downfall came at the Old Bailey, London's infamous criminal court, a cramped and airless building notorious for its ability to inspire despair in defendant and judge alike. After two years of hard labour came Paris: the boulevards, the café terraces, the hotel rooms, and, in 1900, a pauper's grave at Bagneux. London and Paris: for many, Wilde's life is a tale of two cities. There is little room for Dublin in this version of his story, despite the recent efforts that have been made to celebrate Oscar in the city of his birth. In Dublin, Wilde is a ghost twice over.

If Wilde's Dublin days get short shrift in the popular imagination, then there is even less room for Enniskillen. It is true that there is not much to go on. Wilde himself was uncharacteristically tight-lipped about his seven years at Portora Royal School, situated in Enniskillen, County Fermanagh. The school closed down in 2016, but the building that Wilde knew between 1864 and 1871 is still there. An assemblage of austere, graphite-coloured boxes, Portora perches on a little hill above Lough Erne. Other pupils called Wilde 'Grey Crow.' That nickname would do very well for the school itself. It is a bleak and cold place, where high Georgian windows look out over dark water. The school's almost theatrically dour character seems better suited to a later pupil, Samuel Beckett, who studied there between 1920 and 1923. Yes, Portora is more Molloy than Earnest.

Wilde seems to have taken little from Portora apart from a knowledge of Greek and Latin, but a boy of his gifts would have acquired that knowledge wherever he had gone to school. He certainly learned nothing about Ireland at Portora, which seemed to operate under the pretence that it was sited in Oxfordshire rather than Fermanagh—English history was the only history. Nor was there much relief outside the classroom. Extracurricular activities suited to a boy like Oscar were thin on the ground. Even the opportunities for sexual experimentation that supposedly abound at boarding schools seem to have passed him by. No wonder that in later life Wilde would revise his time at school down from seven years to one. When he was convicted of gross indecency in 1895, the authorities at Portora revised his time down even further, from seven years to none. His name was removed from the school's Honours Board. The letters O. W., which he had carved into a windowsill as a boy, were scraped away by the headmaster.

The removal of this childish graffito is particularly affecting. That the masters were aware of it at all in a large school, a building presumably scrimshawed with scratches and doodles made by generations of bored boys, is telling. Those letters on the windowsill were a part of school history for a while. They had been made by a boy who had gone on to do great things. But the boy had gone too far in the end. The school's history had to be scraped back, given a fresh lick of paint.

Portora was not a glamorous start to Wilde's life. It was a dun seven years that even he could not be bothered to mythologise. Instead he minimised his schoolboy years, and succeeded in doing so. But there was one part of his Irish childhood that would follow Wilde across the sea to England. A tiny part of his childhood, admittedly. The merest scintilla of his youth. Yet this was a figure from Oscar's past who would prove instrumental in his downfall, though few now remember Sir Edward Carson for that reason.

He is better known as the man who created Northern Ireland.

The facts of Wilde's downfall are so well known that a brief summary will suffice. He met Lord Alfred Douglas in 1891. Douglas was beautiful, narcissistic, and bored. Wilde never looked back. By 1893, the pair were inseparable. Douglas's father, the Marquess of Queensberry, became increasingly agitated by his son's association with London's foremost dandy. Things came to a head when Queensberry left a card for Wilde at his club in February 1895. The card read: 'For Oscar Wilde, posing as a somdomite [sic].' *Posing* is the key word. It meant that Queensberry could insult Wilde without being prosecuted for libel—he was not accusing Wilde of *being* a sodomite, but of *posing* as one. Being a sodomite was a crime, posing as one was not. Perhaps the misspelling of *sodomite* was a defence of the same kind—accusing a man of 'somdomy' could hardly be considered libellous—though from what is known of Queensberry's intellectual capacity, it is more likely that he simply could not spell the word.

Despite the card's careful phrasing, Wilde sued Queensberry for libel. This was against the advice of many of his friends. The card was insulting, but it had been a personal insult delivered from one man to another. There was no danger of Queensberry's accusation reaching wider society unless Oscar chose to publicise it by taking legal action. And the court-room was no place for a man like Wilde, even as the injured party. His very private life left him vulnerable to counterattack.

Edward Carson was approached to defend Queensberry. Initially, he demurred. Like Wilde, he had been born in Dublin in 1854. They had played together as children on holidays in County Water-ford, and the two men had attended Trinity College at the same time. They had bumped into one another once or twice in London over the years, though they were never friends. Carson felt that this prior associa-tion with Wilde, however slight, presented a conflict of interest. He would not defend a man accused of libelling one of his acquaintances, especially a man like Queensberry, an oafish buffoon whose one dis-tinction in life was having been an enthusiastic pro-ponent of cremation.

Carson changed his mind when it became clear that Queensberry's allegations could be definitively proved in court. Rent boys had been tracked down, witness statements taken, gifts from Oscar to his amours seized as evidence. This change of heart is intriguing. No doubt the reality of Oscar's many liaisons shocked the deeply religious lawyer into action. Equally, it seems arguable that Carson had initially refused the case because he did not think it possible to win: Wilde's prose and plays exhibited a decadent sensibility and a queer approach to morality, but this was nowhere near enough to prove that Queensberry was correct to call him a sodomite. Now that the labyrinth of Wilde's private world had been mapped, the marquess's acquittal seemed certain.

Edward Carson's cross-examination was a sensation. Wilde's wit, charm, and talent for outrageous (though formulaic) paradox were no match for Carson's dogged questioning. His very first sally was a victory. Wilde had stated to the court that he was thirty-eight. Carson, who knew that Wilde had been born in the same year as himself, reminded the playwright that he must be at least forty years old. A small moment, but it mattered. Wilde had perjured himself. Later came the questions about the boys. Did Mr Wilde recognise this name? And this name? And *this* name? And had he given this boy a cigarette case, and that boy a new suit of clothes and a silver-topped cane? Why had he done that? Why, Mr Wilde? Why, why, why?

Wilde's wit faltered. The paradoxes were replaced by desperate little quips. Spectators in the courtroom had laughed along with him at first. Now they eyed him coldly. On the third day of the trial, Wilde's barrister dropped the case against Queensberry. It has been said that Wilde had to seek his fortune in England for the simple reason that the Irish are not impressed by clever talk. In the end, perhaps it was inevitable that a fellow Irishman would be the one to run him to earth.

Today, Edward Carson is remembered for something quite different. His statue stands in front of Northern Ireland's seat of government at Stormont. The bronze statue is raised on a stone dais and presides over the long avenue that leads up to the Parliament buildings. Carson has been captured at the climax of some great speech. One arm is raised, the silent mouth open in an eternal shout. The effect is bellicose, triumphant. It might seem strange, a Dublin man remembered here, outside the enormous stone building that once represented the triumph of Ulster Unionism, until you discover that Edward Carson did more than anyone to bring that bitter victory about.

The debates about Home Rule are often described as a spectre, a spectre that haunted political life in Ireland and England for decades. Home Rule certainly haunted the political careers of successive English prime ministers. In 1886, William Gladstone's third premiership ended in disaster after only four months when his introduction of the First Home Rule Bill for Ireland split his own party down the middle. A second attempt was quashed by the House of Lords in 1893. The matter would not die. This was the subject that Albert Lewis and his friends discussed so interminably in the evenings at Little Lea. Should Ireland remain a part of the United Kingdom, as Protestants like Lewis wished, or should it gain powers of self-governance, though under British supervision? Both nations were split. The prosperous middle classes in Dublin and Belfast favoured the status quo, while an Irish Nationalist tradition stretching back for centuries pressed for Home Rule as a stepping stone to true independence. In England, the Conservatives denounced any attempt to devolve powers to Ireland, while the Liberal Party vacillated between Unionism and Home Rule.

Edward Carson had done very well out of Ireland just the way it was. After taking his law degree at Trinity College, he swiftly made a name for himself as one of the finest lawyers in Dublin. He entered politics and moved to London, continuing to work as a lawyer while serving as a member of Parliament. His confrontation with Wilde in 1895 ended the playwright's career, but Carson's was just beginning. He was a passionate Unionist, and fought tooth and claw against Home Rule in Parliament.

He also fought against it on the ground. Ulster was the heart of Irish Unionism, and that was where Carson expended his energy. Together with other prominent Unionists—notably James Craig, a politician who organised the smuggling of vast quantities of weapons into Ulster from Kaiser Wilhelm's Germany—Carson fought against the increasing likelihood of Home Rule. Carson and Craig organised and equipped tens of thousands of men in the North, a paramilitary body designed as a bulwark against any attempt from Westminster to abandon Protestant Unionists, something frustrated English politicians seemed increasingly likely to do. This organisation was christened the Ulster Volunteer Force, or UVF.

In the end, world events overtook Edward Carson. The First World War eroded the British state's capacity to hold on in Ireland, and its brutal response to the Easter Rising of 1916 destroyed what little good faith remained among the Irish people. Home

Rule, an idea that had once seemed impossibly radical to many, was now nowhere near radical enough. Only a free Ireland would do.

In 1920, the Government of Ireland Act recognised Ireland's independence. The proviso was that staunchly Unionist Ulster should be able to choose her own way. The British government had seen the tide turning, and so the question of partition had already been discussed in private. Now it would have to be implemented. Edward Carson regarded this as a failure. He had wanted to keep Ireland within the United Kingdom whole and entire. Instead he found that he had presided over the creation of a strange new country, a Protestant statelet that no one could have envisioned at the turn of the century.

Both men got their monuments in the end. A plaque was erected to Oscar Wilde at 21 Westland Row, his birthplace. In 1997, a statue was erected on Merrion Square, referred to by local wits as 'the queer fellow.' It shows Wilde reclining on a rock, relaxing beneath the trees. There is a plaque to him now at Portora too. Wilde's old school still stands grey above Lough Erne. Carson's border is just ten miles away.

CHAPTER FOUR

Genius but no education

I come from haunts of coot and hern I make a sudden sally and sparkle out among the fern to bicker down a valley...in the name of God and of the dead generations from which she receives her old tradition of nationhood Ireland through us summons her children to her flag and strikes for her freedom...I chatter over stony ways in little sharps and trebles I bubble into eddying bays I babble on the pebbles...haste thee nymph and bring with thee health and youthful jollity she strikes in full confidence of victory...we were in the

reign of Cáhal Mór of the wine-red hand...
cherishing all the children of the nation
equally...and out again I curve and flow to
join the brimming river for men may come
and men may go but I go on forever.

This was what school gave Patrick Kavanagh. Childhood was Lord Tennyson and John Milton and James
Clarence Mangan. He left school at thirteen and
these lines followed him into the fields. They were
his first poems. Other lines came too, inescapable in
those days, the swell and roll of the Proclamation of
the Irish Republic.

Patrick Kavanagh was born in 1904 in a place
called Mucker. Mucker was a mile from the village of
Inniskeen in County Monaghan. Things could have
been worse. Patrick's father was a cobbler and had
done well enough to rebuild the family home and to
buy a nine-acre farm for two hundred pounds. Some
Dublin poets would have called them peasants. But
the Kavanaghs owned their land and could rely upon
an essential trade—everyone needs shoes. No money
to spare, but food on the table.

He worked in the fields. He thinned turnips and
fed pigs. His father tried to teach him how to make
shoes. It did not take. He began to write. Every

evening he would sit in a corner of his cold bedroom and make poems. There were no books. Nothing to go on. Only the poems that he had read in school. Impossible to imagine now. That you could be sixty miles from Dublin and have nothing to read but an old anthology from your schooldays, filled with poems from another time and another place. Tennyson's 'The Brook', Scott's *Lady of the Lake*, Milton's 'L'Allegro'. Nineteenth century, or seventeenth, and all of it from Britain. After Patrick died a television crew went to interview the clientele at his favourite pub, McDaid's. There one of his drinking buddies declaimed a verse from Thomas Gray's 'Elegy Written in a Country Churchyard': 'Some village-Hampden, that with dauntless breast / The little tyrant of his fields withstood; / Some mute inglorious Milton here may rest, / Some Cromwell guiltless of his country's blood.'

Patrick had taught it to him.

Ireland was at war between 1919 and 1923. First the War of Independence from 1919 to 1921, then the Civil War from 1922 to 1923. Nasty, bitter struggles. A family feud that spilled out of houses and twisted along country roads. There was never the luxury of a no-man's-land. The enemy was in the pub, across the street, on the other side of the hedgerow. Patrick's brother would later write that 'fortunately for Patrick he was too young to become involved with either. Not that he would have, had he been older: Father would not have allowed it. We were never involved in politics.'

The politics of day-to-day life were another matter entirely. Everyone in the North was political from the moment they were born. Names were political, land was political. Patrick grew up knowing that there were people who were not like him. Even a pilgrimage to a holy well was complicated. The well was on land owned by a Protestant clergyman, who would lock the gate so Catholic pilgrims had to scramble over a thorny hedge to bottle the sacred water welling up from the earth.

This was the way the North had been for generations. A writer from another time told much the same stories. William Carleton was born in County Tyrone in 1794 and died in 1869, thirty-five years before Patrick was born. Like Patrick he was a Catholic writer from the North, and like Patrick he described conflict between Catholics and Protestants as one might mention a toothache to a friend. When William was a boy, the little town of Augher decided to put on a play. Not just any play. They chose *The Battle of Aughrim*. This was an historical drama about the battle of 1691 at which William of Orange finally defeated James II. Catholic residents of Augher would play the Jacobites and Protestants the Williamites. Young Carleton helped the men to learn their lines. He cannot have been overly shocked when this drama descended into farce: 'When they came to the conflict with which the play is made to close, armed as they were on both sides with real swords, political and religious resentment could not be restrained, and they would have hacked each other's souls out had not the audience interfered and prevented them. As it was, some of them were severely if not dangerously wounded.'

These were the stories that everyone heard when young. This was the way life was structured. Patrick's brother may have been right to say that his family as a whole was not political, but he was disingenuous when it came to Patrick. Patrick had opinions. And he had the young man's disease: 'I wanted a fight. I had missed the Black and Tan scrap and now it seemed we were in for the monotony of peace.' The Black and Tan scrap was the War of Independence. Patrick would enjoy a sort of peace in the following years, but the monotony was broken from time to time. On some nights he would go out and run with the IRA.

Mucker, isolated Mucker, was as divided by the Civil War as anywhere else. On the one side were the Free Staters, who supported the treaty made with Great Britain in 1921. Ireland would govern itself but become a dominion of the British Empire. Furthermore, it gave the six counties of Northern Ireland the choice between the Irish Free State and Great Britain. Northern Ireland duly opted out of the Free State. Overnight, the island of Ireland was partitioned. The new border was just three miles from Mucker. For many the treaty was a betrayal, a sleight of hand. Ireland was either a free and sovereign nation or it was not.

The IRA waged a guerrilla campaign against the Free State, and Patrick claimed that he had joined them from time to time. He was never an official member, but he would go out and cut telegraph wires. Once he tried to hold up a train. Holding up trains had been elevated to a county sport by the 1920s. Patrick and his comrades tripped the red light that would signal the train to halt, only for the locomotive to race past them at thirty-five miles an hour: 'What had happened was this—the train had already been held up further down the line and a barrel of porter and several chests of tea taken from it. I believe it was tobacco and cigarettes we were after.'

He got in other scrapes too: a failed attempt to bomb the homes of two Free Staters, a spot of burglary from the local Big House.* But Patrick's nocturnal escapades ended with the Civil War. He sat on his cobbler's bench under his father's gaze, or worked out in the fields from dawn to dusk, or perched on a bag of oats and made poems.

Years passed. This is where Patrick's isolation tells. The years spent alone in his head without a guide. Not wasted years by any means. This was the time that would feed his work for the rest of his life. Work and earth and place. And then the world came to Patrick Kavanagh and showed him what he had been missing. The world arrived in 1927, and it was folded inside the pages of a magazine found in a Dundalk newsagent's:

'What kind of a paper is this?' I asked the newsagent.

'Something like *John Bull*,' he said.

It was the *Irish Statesman* ... I opened the paper and read.

---

* Big House: a term used to describe the stately homes that dotted the Irish countryside. These symbols of colonial rule were burned down in their hundreds during the 1920s. Much of Ireland's finest architecture was destroyed as a result.

The first thing my eye fell upon was a review of a book by Gertrude Stein. I read a quotation and found it like a foreign language, partly illuminated by the Holy Spirit. There was mention of a man named Joyce.

The *Irish Statesman* was edited by a man called George Russell. He had turned it into one of Ireland's foremost literary journals. Patrick's encounter with this paper changed his life. Poetry was something that was being made. It was not an art that had died with Queen Victoria. Poetry was quick, and men in Dublin would take a poem and put it in a paper so that anyone could read it. The *Irish Statesman* gave Patrick a purchase, something to aim at. He began to send poems to George Russell.

First came rejection. Patrick was elated. Rejection was a kind of contact. Someone has to notice you before they can reject you. They have to read your work before they decide how good it is. Patrick was being read by a Dublin editor.

It took him two years, but he did it. In 1929, Russell accepted three of Patrick's poems for publication. These poems are not vintage Kavanagh. But the seed is there. One of the poems that appeared in the *Irish Statesman* was called 'Ploughman'. It begins:

I turn the lea-green down
Gaily now,
And paint the meadow brown
With my plough.

I dream with silvery gull
And brazen crow.
A thing that is beautiful
I may know . . .

The poem is work. Painful labour that racks the back and turns palms to driftwood. The Kavanagh twist comes with the plough as paintbrush and the meadow as canvas. He knew art in his life. Soon enough, Dublin would see art in him.

* * *

Kavanagh walked to Dublin to see George Russell. This was in December 1931. Russell was a poet himself. He spent a time writing under the pseudonym Æon. Perhaps he came to see this as pretentious, perhaps he decided that it was two letters too long. Either way he started writing as plain Æ and that is how he is still remembered.

Æ sported a famous beard. Descriptions of the man always mention his beard. It was a wild and

vigorous growth that might have earned an approv-
ing nod from Rasputin. Perhaps it was the most
famous beard in Dublin. When people weren't calling George Russell Æ, they were calling him the
hairy fairy. The 'fairy' part was more than a pleas-
ing rhyme. Æ was a mystic who believed marvel-
lous things. As a young man he had read Madame
Blavatsky and lived above the Dublin Theosophi-
cal Society. He knew James Joyce and was one of
W. B. Yeats's closest friends. He painted strange pictures of radiant women towering over whitewashed
cottages. His collections of poetry had titles like *The
Earth Breath*, *The Divine Vision*, *The House of Titans*.
He believed that Mother Ireland spoke to her people
through the land:

> A true national culture is an emanation from
> the Earth spirit, a voice speaking directly to
> the dwellers in that land generation after gen-
> eration so that from many visions the earth
> becomes sacred, hills, rivers, mountains,
> lakes are all transparencies through which the
> divine world is seen. Ireland, Greece, India
> still have traditions going back to the foun-
> dations of the world.

This was the man that Patrick Kavanagh had walked sixty miles to see. Literary history is full of great walks. Arthur Rimbaud's walk from Charleville to Paris, Walt Whitman's walk from New York City to his wounded brother, Robert Louis Stevenson's stroll through the Cévennes, Patrick Leigh Fermor's walk from Rotterdam to Constantinople. There can be few creatures on this earth more self-aware than a writer on a long walk, and Kavanagh was no exception. He knew what Æ expected of the man who had written 'Ploughman'. His walk to Dublin was preparation of the kind that an actor would recognise. He had a part to play and he intended to play it well.

Kavanagh dressed in his battered work jacket and trousers that bore 'the tramp-necessary rectangular knee patches.' He wore hobnailed boots that he had made himself, an ominous admission given that he never mastered the cobbling trade. His pockets contained three shillings and fourpence halfpenny and a journal that he could not be bothered to keep up.

He begged on the road—a cup of tea here, a crust of stale bread there. Kavanagh could not afford to do otherwise and yet his hunger was counterfeit, ludicrous. He was always the butt of his own joke. His account of those days of walking is black comedy.

A blacksmith thought Kavanagh more of a school-master than a tramp. One woman gave him tea and looked him over:

> 'Yer not a tramp,' she said.
> 'To my grief I am,' I replied.
> 'Yer up to some cod-actin',' she declared.
> 'I'd know a real tramp.'

In Dublin he went to the National Library of Ireland to ask for Æ's address. The black comedy continued. The librarians did not know where Æ lived but offered up the address of Oliver St. John Gogarty. Kavanagh was not impressed. His mood darkened further when he asked for a copy of T. S. Eliot's 'The Waste Land' and was shown a selection of books on drainage.

This episode is peculiar. Kavanagh had been published by Æ and had corresponded with him. He could have written to Æ, told him of his planned visit to Dublin, and asked for his address directly. Maybe he did so, but of course this would mean dispens-ing with the incident at the National Library, which would have been a loss of artistic truth. And it is quite possible that things fell out the way he said that they did. Kavanagh was a theatrical man and keenly aware of how Æ could best be charmed. Arranging an appointment was urban, bourgeois. The country people that Æ feted came into a house and sat down by the stove without a word.

Eventually Kavanagh found Æ's home. He wrote of his reception there: 'He appeared quite certain that I was a beggar. I regretted not having a fiddle under my arm to add a touch of wild colour to my drab tramp.' For a moment it seemed that his cod-acting had been all too successful. He had overdone things. But he had only to say his name for Æ to welcome this rural genius inside.

There, in that Dublin drawing room, Kavanagh regretted his patched trousers and hobnailed boots. If Æ noticed them, he gave no sign. He was mourning the death of his wife, Violet, and was naturally distracted. But he rallied. He spoke of Whitman and Emerson and loaded Kavanagh down with their collected works, as well as literary periodicals, *Les Misérables*, *The Idiot*, *The Brothers Karamazov*, and collections of poetry, including some of his own. Four stone of books, reckoned Kavanagh. He left Æ's home knowing that the man had 'opened the door to me, and not merely the door of wood on his house in Rathgar.'

Publishing the unknown Kavanagh had been Æ's

first act of generosity. Kavanagh's visit prompted a second one. Æ began to talk up his Monaghan man in letters to Yeats:

> There is plenty of talent in Ireland today if there were people willing to take trouble to help half-educated young men to find themselves. There is a young shoemaker in Monaghan who has genius but no education. I unloaded three dozen books on him ranging from Dostoevsky to philosophy, and he is in a state of ferment, the only things apart from magazines he had read.

To visit Æ was an obvious move from a young poet on the make. Being published was all very well, but then as now, this was no substitute for spending time with an editor who could spread your name around at the right parties. And Æ was more than willing to do just this. He was from Lurgan in County Armagh, and perhaps he was especially keen to sing the praises of a fellow northerner. But there is no doubt that, above all else, Æ valued Kavanagh as a poet. Not only for the quality of the verse, but for what a man like Kavanagh meant to him. To understand what Kavanagh meant to Æ, you have to know what the aging editor had spent his life doing, and to know about that, you have to look at his friendship with William Butler Yeats.

Yeats and Æ met at the Art Schools in Dublin in 1884 and remained friends for the rest of their lives. They were both apprentice mystics searching for the same Ireland.

In 1893 the young Yeats wrote a book about faeries. He called it *The Celtic Twilight*. It is full of good stories: the faeries who force a youth to turn a corpse on a spit ('if you let it burn we'll have to put you on the spit instead'); the old man who pulls his chimney down because of the faery that sits upon it playing interminable pipe music all night long; the black-hooded sorcerers who summon spectral snakes with an Arabic invocation. Yet while the book concerns faeries, it lingers on humans. The men and women who spoke of the Good People are the real heroes of *The Celtic Twilight*. As Yeats saw it, 'To the wise peasant the green hills and woods round him are full of never-fading mystery.' He glorified these 'peasants' and was keen to place himself among them: 'One night as I sat eating Mrs. H—'s soda bread, her husband told me a longish story'. The book opens

with Paddy Flynn, an old man who had seen the ban-
shee 'batting the river with its hands' and who pos-
sessed 'the visionary melancholy of purely instinctive
natures and of all animals.'

The Celtic Twilight was a form of claiming. Ireland could be found in the speech of these instinctive natures. Ireland *was* the instinctive nature. The
true Ireland, the eternal country that England had
never touched, could never have touched. This was
the Ireland that would quicken again when the land
was free. Yeats was not alone with his fey thoughts.
A whole generation of Irish writers went in search of
the true Ireland, certain only that it was to be found
somewhere on the margins, on the Aran Islands or in
a whitewashed cottage, or maybe, just maybe, on a
small farm in County Monaghan.

Artists are the first to call for revolution and the
first to be disappointed by it. The establishment of
the Irish state certainly disappointed men like Æ and
Yeats. They were confronted by the realisation that
not everyone in Ireland thought as they did. Hop-
ing for a rejuvenation of the Irish soul, they were
instead given the Committee on Evil Literature, a
five-man body which, unusually for government
committees, had the decency to be unambiguous
in its aims. Backed by a resurgent Catholic Church,

the committee recommended a severe tightening of Irish obscenity law. The result was the foundation of the Censorship of Publications Board in 1929. At a stroke, Ireland became one of the most censorious countries in western Europe. Newspapers, novels, and films were all subject to review and suppression. The censors were nothing if not diligent. They banned books by James Joyce and Samuel Beckett and John McGahern. The slightest whiff of muck or satire was quashed with overwhelming force.

Æ despaired. In 1932 he wrote a letter to Yeats saying, 'I feel alien to everything except the earth itself and if it was not for that love I would leave Ireland.' The world that he had hoped for had died in the cradle. Ireland now seemed 'like a lout I knew in boyhood who had become a hero and then subsided into a lout again.'

Yeats tried to fight back. In concert with George Bernard Shaw, he founded the Irish Academy of Letters, which aimed to mobilise the nation's writers against the censors. In this it failed. The academy became a running joke as the years went by, regarded even by its members as a pretty shambolic institution. Louis MacNeice was invited to join in 1939. He accepted, but admitted to his wife that 'the Irish Academy of Letters meets once a year in Dublin's only decent restaurant and gets so drunk they have to send the waiters away.'

The academy was not wholly useless. It offered prizes for young writers, and in 1932, in the midst of his gloom, Æ thought that he had found a worthy winner for the first award: 'I have hopes that we may have a new young genius ready for the first prize—a small farmer from Monaghan, whose verses have a wild & original fire in them. I discovered him first, & Frank O'Connor thinks his verse is very splendid.'

'I discovered him first'. Æ had published two of Kavanagh's poems in the *Irish Statesman*. This was the first prominent journal to publish his work, and in that sense the hairy fairy was right to say that he had discovered Kavanagh. But there is another way to read that sentence. Æ didn't name Kavanagh in his letter to Yeats. The man's name wasn't the point. The point was the dirt under his nails and his 'wild & original fire'.

A Monaghan farmer-poet was uniquely vulnerable to being *discovered* by Dublin literati. He was a picturesque figure whether he liked it or not, the uneducated peasant inspired to verse, the man of the soil linking couplets at his plough. The cod-acting had paid off: Kavanagh was quaint. More, he was useful. He confirmed romantic notions about the unique spirituality of the Irish earth and the Irish soul just when they were needed most. Here was the instinctive nature, here was Ireland. A tall man living quietly in the North with genius but no education.

He was twenty-six years old and on his way.

CHAPTER FIVE

The lamp was dark beside my bed

I rish poetry was born in darkness. Four hundred years ago, poets were trained in lightless rooms. The technique was so effective—and so steeped in tradition—that most poets continued to compose in the pitch black throughout their lives. This is the way poems in the Irish language were made for centuries.

Poetic education was conducted during the winter months, in some out-of-the-way place where the master and his students would not be disturbed. First, a subject was given to the apprentice poets. This subject was more than a simple theme, such as the praise of a local lord or the description of a place. The master expected his students to compose according to exacting rules, chiefly those which governed any number of particular syllabic metres. These metres dictated how many syllables should appear in each line, with special attention given to the final word in each. Mastery of these metres was essential to the poetic life.

Such command of metre took six or seven seasons of study. It is easy to see why. Alliteration, stress, accents. All were carefully formalised. Even rhyming was a minefield. An aural rhyme was not good enough. The words in a poem had to 'rhyme' grammatically too, in adherence to strict conventions that dictated which consonants could chime with one another. While William Shakespeare could match 'days' with 'praise', an Irish poet did not have this luxury. As the scholar James Carney put it: 'What in English would be regarded as full rhyme, in Irish would often be felt as a breach of good style.'

These technical considerations were just the beginning. More general stylistic conventions were also enforced. The last words of a poem would ideally echo the opening line, so as to create a sense of satisfaction as the poem closed. Impressionistic use of the Irish language was encouraged. And as with all good poetry, brevity was all. The ability to build an allusive word picture with concision and flair was highly prized.

Subject in heads, the students retired to a windowless hut. Beds were spaced at regular intervals inside, often screened off from one another to form small chambers within the building. The students would lie down in the dark. In 1722, the Marquis of Clanricarde described what happened next: 'The said subject having been given overnight, they work'd it apart each by himself upon his own bed, the whole next day in the dark, till at a certain hour in the night, lights being brought in, they committed it to writing.'

Darkness permitted slow and careful gestation. The marquis described a span of time—night, day, night again—which could have been twenty-four hours or more. Necessary time. The demands placed on those young poets were severe. This was mind work, nib-less drawing on eyelids. Each syllable had to be weighed. Every line was a course of brickwork to be mortared and dismantled again. Imagine the despair when a witty opening had to be discarded, or a curling image clipped to fit metrical convention. Hours lost murmuring into the void. The knowledge that your fellows were working too, wondering what quatrains they were building from their narrow beds. It was dark in the poets' hut, but it cannot have been silent. Rain on the thatch. Wind beyond the walls. Mice skittering. The sudden rush of a filling chamber pot. Bellies would have rumbled, soft curses been uttered. And sleep must have been a danger. If you heard a man snoring, did you rise from your pallet to shake him? Or leave him to snooze, waiting for the moment he would wake in a panic, measuring his lost time in syllables? Perhaps the cold helped the young poets to stay awake. They trained in the winter, after all, and a warming fire was unthinkable in the gloomy hut.

The dark guaranteed concentration, but there was more to it than that. Status was gained from this gruelling and unusual education. Those lightless seasons of study were the sacrifice young men made to become poets. Even today, at a remove of centuries, these night-verses resonate. It has been suggested that the practice 'must have owed its origin to some pagan custom that prevailed when the poet was both magician and seer.' This may well be so, but such speculation is unwarranted when the symbolic charge of creation in darkness is so clear. Christian lyrics formed a large part of these poets' repertoire, and the concept of creation from the void must have been familiar to them. More mundane associations occur as well. A comparison to the womb is obvious, as is the suggestion of the cave. An unknowing return to man's distant past. Ochre handprints on stone.

The young men who undertook this course of study were training to be bards. They hoped to attract the patronage of a lord who would give them land and security. In return, they would compose verses that counted his virtues, celebrated his lineage, and satirised his enemies. The promise of wealth and favour meant that bards were willing to sing for their supper in any hall that would have them. Since arriviste lords of Anglo-Norman stock had just as much largesse to dispense as the old Irish nobility, bards became used to tailoring poems to their audience. In the fourteenth century, the celebrated poet Gofraidh Fionn Ó Dálaigh cheerfully admitted that 'in poetry to the English we promise that the Irish will be exiled from Ireland, and in poems to the Irish we vow that the English will be driven across the sea to the East.'

The students lying in those dark huts were destined for careers in noble households and were always from aristocratic backgrounds themselves. It was a family trade. Bards tended to be the sons of bards. They were as proud of their lineage as any earl, and guarded their privileges jealously. Gruelling training and painstaking mastery of syllabic metre gave bards status. That status had to be protected. Fear Flatha Ó Gnímh was bard to the O'Neills, one of Ulster's most ancient noble families. In one poem, Ó Gnímh boasted that he would never compose a poem 'without secrecy and darkness,' while reclining on 'the beds where prize lyrics are made.' The poem was addressed to Fearghal Óg, a man who was said to compose his poetry on horseback. To write poems in the open air was bad enough, but to do so while riding a horse was an unimaginable vulgarity. Real poems were fitted together by aristocrats in dark huts. As Ó Gnímh wrote, 'I like a thing which keeps me from error—a barrier to keep out the sunlight, and dim couches to guard me.' Rival poetic traditions—free verse written on horseback, for example—were ruthlessly satirised. Men like Ó Gnímh had to remind their noble patrons that true poetry belonged to the bards alone. Yet this poem is a sad work, written in the autumn of an ancient tradition. Men like Fearghal Óg were the future.

Fear Flatha Ó Gnímh lived to see the end of it all. He is thought to have died in 1630 and would therefore have lived through the final collapse of the old Irish nobility. In 1602, the armies of Elizabeth I, queen of England, defeated an Irish army at Kinsale after a three-month siege of the town. The Battle of

Kinsale was the last gasp of an uprising that began in
Ulster in 1594. That rebellion was led by Ó Gnímh's
patron, Hugh O'Neill, Earl of Tyrone. Although
O'Neill returned to Ulster after his defeat at Kinsale, he took ship from Lough Swilly in 1607. Rory
O'Donnell, Earl of Tyrconnell, went with him. The
earls never returned. Other nobles followed suit over
the coming years, and those who stayed in Ireland
gradually lost their land and authority. The Flight of
the Earls, as it came to be known, marked the beginning of the end of bardic culture. When the old lords
of Ireland fled to Spain or France, they took their
patronages with them. The intricate poetry that
bards laboured in the dark to master had lost its audience forever.

Another Ulster bard, Eochaidh Ó Heóghusa, was
court poet to the Maguires of Fermanagh. It fell to
him to adapt to a changing world and to the tastes
that changed with it. He described his experiments
with 'free verse on the open road.' Abandoning his
dark hut, he had 'gone out in the rain like the rest—
a wise course.' Once he had worked for weeks on
poems that were erudite, complex, and obscure.
Now 'artlessness and softness' were preferable to
'carven ornament'—the writer's writer had gone
commercial. Still, if you can't beat them, counselled

Ó Heóghusa, you might as well join them. And it wasn't all bad. There were advantages to free verse on the open road: 'Every poem I composed hitherto used almost to break my heart: this new fashion that has come to us is a great cause for health.'

*　*　*

Poems no longer came from the dark. But darkness continued to birth poets. In 1907, three hundred years after the Flight of the Earls, Louis MacNeice was born in Belfast. He grew up in Carrickfergus, on the north shore of Belfast Lough. The town kneels around a Norman castle. The castle is a simple building, a squat keep girdled by a curtain wall. No fancy turrets or concentric fortifications here. Carrickfergus Castle has a blunt and workmanlike air. It was thrown up in 1177 by John de Courcy, the first Norman to lay claim to land in Ulster, and continued to offer protection to the people of Carrickfergus right up to the Second World War, when it was used as an air raid shelter. It was built to command the tiny harbor that leads out to the lough. A harsh place in winter, but in summer calm the water is still as setting glue, stretching away to the green of the lough's southern shore.

Louis's father, John, was a Protestant clergyman.

He was appointed rector of St Nicholas' Church in Carrickfergus in 1908, and Louis grew up in the comfortable rectory that came with the appointment. Lily, his mother, was never happy there. The congregation of St Nicholas' didn't want John MacNeice as rector, and the family was ostracised by the community at first. Naturally, the new rector's wife bore the brunt of this cold welcome. She organised tea parties that no one from the parish would attend. The locals were not the only problem. Lily was from County Galway, and she missed the west of Ireland deeply. Worse, her health was poor and getting poorer. In 1913 she was sent to Dublin for treatment. Although expected to recover, she never returned to Carrickfergus. Lily MacNeice died in December 1914, a week before Christmas. Louis was seven years old.

Thirty-six years later, in September 1940, Louis wrote a poem called 'Autobiography':

In my childhood trees were green
And there was plenty to be seen.

Come back early or never come.

My father made the walls resound,
He wore his collar the wrong way round.

Come back early or never come.

My mother wore a yellow dress;
Gentle, gently, gentleness.

Come back early or never come.

When I was five the black dreams came;
Nothing after was quite the same.

Come back early or never come.

The dark was talking to the dead;
The lamp was dark beside my bed.

Come back early or never come.

When I woke they did not care;
Nobody, nobody was there.

Come back early or never come.

When my silent terror cried,
Nobody, nobody replied.

Come back early or never come.

I got up; the chilly sun
Saw me walk away alone.

Come back early or never come.

This is a story of childhood, and the simple language comes from a child's mouth. 'Autobiography' is a macabre lullaby. The green trees, the father practising his sermons, the mother in a yellow dress: all are eaten by the dark. '*Come back early or never come*', a refrain that could be the title of a ghost story by M. R. James, grows ever more appalling as it is repeated. The 'black dreams' arrived when Louis was five, his age at the time of his mother's departure for Dublin in August 1913. She failed to come back early, despite the expectations of her family. She never came back at all.

Louis wrote many different kinds of autobiography. The most traditional is *The Strings Are False*, a book he began in 1939 and never finished. In it he describes his childhood with tactile care, as if he were running his hand up the bannisters of the rectory once again. Like Forrest Reid, MacNeice found that his home was a haunted place. The problem was that 'things project other things.' Louis was imaginative, perhaps too much so. He made connections that other children would not. He saw the sinister potential that lurked within every action. His mother would come to the nursery in the evening and use her hands to cast 'rabbits' on the lamplit walls. The shadowy animals disappeared when his mother dropped her hands, but Louis was haunted by a troubling thought. What if the rabbits *didn't* disappear when his mother said good night and went downstairs? What if they *stayed*? There was much else to fear. John MacNeice intoning prayers alone in his study; the strange brown stain that the oil lamp made on the ceiling. The cook's riddle was particularly terrifying:

> And Annie the cook had a riddle which began 'What is it that goes round and round the house?' And the answer was the wind but, though I knew that was the answer in the riddle, I had a clammy suspicion that in fact it might be something else. Going round and round the house, evil, waiting to get me.

Yet nothing was worse than the black dreams. They were formless, terrifying. Not bad dreams relating to a situation—the tiger that wants to have you for lunch—but a state: 'There was a kind of a noise that I felt rather than heard, "ah...ah...ah," a grey monotonous rhythm which drew me in towards a centre as if there were a spider at the centre drawing in his thread and everything else were unreal.'

The unreal. It is no accident that MacNeice's poetry is concerned with definite things. He did not dabble in abstract woo-woo. He knew how a particular room smelled, how heavy an object was. He wanted to understand what he saw. When he watched snow falling through a window, he wanted to know how that experience *worked*, and he wrote a poem to find out. In his study of W. B. Yeats, he emphasised the importance of what he called 'thinghood'— poems were as definite as a budgie in a cage. But things project other things, and MacNeice's poetry of things projects unsettling shapes on the wall. Projection requires a surface, a source of light, and something in between. That something in between might be a cel of film, or a hand, or a poem.

Like C. S. Lewis, MacNeice was sent to school in England. First to Sherborne, then Marlborough. His time at the latter school was significant. He fell in with a bookish, aesthetically minded crowd. The most important of these friendships was with a boy called Anthony Blunt. Blunt would spend his life writing scholarly books on Nicolas Poussin, lecturing at the Courtauld Institute of Art, and holding the office of surveyor of the queen's pictures. Despite these achievements, he is now best known as one of the Cambridge Spies, a group of five young men who passed British intelligence to the Soviet Union during the war.

Blunt had a profound effect on the young Mac-Neice: 'Thanks awfully for introducing me to Art,' he wrote in one letter, though doubtless with his tongue firmly in cheek. His letters to Blunt were written in an affected and self-consciously intellectual register designed to amuse. Life in Carrickfergus during the holidays was dissected: 'The family is just like a bad Tchekov play...My father reads the Bible in his bath.' Fashionable authors of the time were trashed: 'Have just read such a bad novel by Ernest Hemingway one of those tiresome Parisian Americans.' And once MacNeice arrived at Merton College, Oxford, his fellow undergraduates were ruthlessly pilloried: 'Stuck once more among all the mudfaced abortions & cyphers & dullards & frogspawn—Might God engulf them in a yawning nullity.'

Blunt and MacNeice remained close until the mid-1930s, when they seem to have drifted apart. MacNeice had married and was juggling family, career, and poetry, while Blunt is thought to have been recruited by the KGB around this time. Blunt's tragedy was to allow an adolescent posture—Marxism of the most naive and modish variety—to form his adult life. Marxism never held much allure for Mac-Neice. He was not one for systems. As Edna Longley has observed, his Ulster childhood had made him suspicious of revolutionary fervour. Eruptions of violence in Ireland were always justified with one manifesto or another. This was especially true of the North, where Protestant anxiety over 'the enemy within' often took violent form. Take July 1920, when the forcible expulsion of thousands of Catholic workers from the shipyards plunged Belfast into two years of vicious riots. MacNeice knew all too well that imagined utopias led to blood in the streets. Unlike Blunt, he had the sense to change and grow.

Awareness of change, of time's rushing stream, is central to his poetry. The ancient Greek philosopher Heraclitus, who stated that 'everything flows', found a willing disciple in MacNeice. In 'Variation on Heraclitus' (1961) he wrote, 'Even the walls are flowing, even the ceiling, / Nor only in terms of physics; the pictures / Bob on each picture rail like floats on a line'. His most famous work, *Autumn Journal*, is a poetic record of the final, febrile months of

1938. The poem takes in the Spanish Civil War, a love affair, London bracing for the Luftwaffe, and meditations on Ireland. A lesson learned from this kaleidoscope is that 'Time is a country, the present moment / A spotlight roving round the scene; / We need not chase the spotlight, / The future is the bride of what has been.'

After school came Oxford and the inevitable classics degree. Then a teaching post at the University of Birmingham, where E. R. Dodds, a distinguished classicist and fellow Ulsterman, took the shy and diffident young scholar under his wing. Although Auden and MacNeice had known one another at Oxford, it was Dodds who brought the two men together, a crucial moment in the mythology of the 'Thirties Poets'. Critics like to think in terms of movements, and Louis MacNeice, Stephen Spender, W. H. Auden, and Cecil Day-Lewis—dubbed 'Macspaunday' by Roy Campbell—made a lovely set, albeit a manufactured one. Auden's talent as a poet and friend must have been helpful to MacNeice, as were the connections that he could provide. In 1940, the pair spent time in New York City together, in a brownstone at 7 Middagh Street. This was the Brooklyn Heights home of George Davis, fiction editor of *Harper's Bazaar*. Other guests included Benjamin Britten, Jane

Bowles, and Carson McCullers. Twenty-three years later, MacNeice would reread all of McCullers's novels during his final illness.

* * *

Louis MacNeice grew into a tall man. He was all angles. His face was long, like the blade of a shovel. Photographs preserve his striking features: the broad escarpment of his forehead and the ridge of his nose. His bottom lip was full, his top lip a hard white line. Contemporaries made much of his laconic character and angular presence. The poet John Hewitt spotted him at the funeral of W. B. Yeats: 'I recognized the long dark head of Louis MacNeice, in his black oilskin coat'. Bob Pocock, a fellow BBC man, remembered the 'bent black safety pin of the eyes and hidalgo curl of the lip.' C. S. Lewis first met MacNeice in 1927, at a party thrown by John Betjeman in Oxford. He thought MacNeice 'absolutely silent and astonishingly ugly.' 'He doesn't say much', said Betjeman. 'But he's a great poet.'

Not everyone displayed Betjeman's indulgence towards the taciturn writer. Stephen Spender described a London party thrown by the publisher John Lehmann during the Second World War. MacNeice spent the whole evening 'leaning back against the chimney piece, and holding a glass in one hand, surveyed the party through half-closed eyes, without addressing a word to anyone.' Another guest—the British ambassador to the Soviet Union, Archibald Clark Kerr—was outraged by this gauche display, and resolved to give MacNeice a piece of his mind. Spender recalled the moment that the ambassador buttonholed the poet:

> Did MacNeice come from the Northern coast of Ireland? MacNeice acknowledged that he did. 'Ah,' said Clark-Kerr, 'well that corroborates a legend I heard in my youth that a school of seals had landed on that part of the coast, cohabited with the natives, and produced a special race, half-seal, half-human.' MacNeice did look a bit taken aback, as Clark-Kerr left the room.

Naturally it was the ambassador who left the party, not MacNeice. Louis MacNeice was never seen walking out of a room. Louis MacNeice never walked into a room either. Even people who knew him well never seemed to see him come or go. Mac-Neice was simply *there*, propped up against a wall or a bookcase, so that one imagines the man silent in the corner of a dark and empty salon, waiting for someone to switch on a lamp and say, 'Oh, hello, Louis. Fancy a drink?'

The novelist Maurice Leitch encountered him at the BBC in Belfast: 'It was a bit disappointing, actually. Sam Hanna Bell who was my friend and mentor said, "Oh you must meet Louis one day," and I was coming down the corridor and there was this angular, tall chap, leaning up against a doorway, and he sort of grunted when I was introduced to him. And that was the only occasion I met him.' Again we find MacNeice in situ, leaning on the nearest vertical, and again he is taciturn, seemingly uninterested. Leitch marked his height and angularity, the slant of him. We have bodies. Louis MacNeice had geometry.

MacNeice's presence outlived him. Spender dreamed about his dead friend on a visit to New York City in 1975. He had been reading Louis's poem 'Bagpipe Music', a bleak and antic work that bemoans the growing thinness of twentieth-century life: 'The glass is falling hour by hour, the glass will fall forever, / But if you break the bloody glass you won't hold up the weather.' One stanza in 'Bagpipe Music' features the word *ceilidh*, a Scots Gaelic term for a traditional dance party. Spender, somewhat surprisingly, did not know what the word meant. Nor did he know how to pronounce it. But he did know how his friend would have reacted to his ignorance: 'I saw Louis standing at the foot of my bed, looking down at me, with amused contempt in his gaze.' The shade of Louis MacNeice inspired a poem:

> *Like skyscrapers with high windows staring*
> > *down from*
> *the sun,*
> *Some faces suggest*
> *Elevation. Their way-up eyes*
> *Look down at you diagonally and their aloof*
> *Hooded glance suggests*
> *A laugh turning somersaults in some high*
> > *penthouse*
> *Of their skulls . . .*
> —'Seeing MacNeice Stand before Me' (1975)

When he wasn't leaning on mantelpieces, he was writing. MacNeice wrote a great deal. My father's 1966 edition of the *Collected Poems*, edited by E. R. Dodds, is over five hundred pages long. The 2007 *Collected Poems*, edited by Peter McDonald, is a doorstop of 880 pages. And the poems weren't the half of it. MacNeice wrote plays and translations and nonfiction. He collaborated with W. H. Auden on a poetic

travelogue, *Letters from Iceland* (1937). His book on
W. B. Yeats remains a classic, and he produced numer-
ous articles and reviews on other literary subjects. But
he would turn his hand to almost anything. On his
death, an unfinished history of astrology was found
among his papers. During the war he dashed off a
pamphlet for British schoolchildren entitled *Meet the
U.S. Army* (1943), which explained what those gum-
chewing men with strange accents were all about.
And in the summer of 1938 he wrote *Zoo*, perhaps his
most unusual work. *Zoo* was not the title of a poetry
collection; it really was a book about zoos, places that
had always fascinated him. Sadly, the *Times Literary
Supplement* dismissed it as a 'go-as-you-please affair'
and a 'deliberately inconsequent work,' although
the reviewer did admire MacNeice's descriptions
of the animals. Yet it is a wonderful book, if only
for the image that it plants in the reader's mind of
Louis MacNeice leaning against the giraffe enclosure
at London Zoo, smoking a cigarette and admiring
the dip and dapple of long necks in the sun.

It has been said that MacNeice did not write much
about Ireland. This is largely an optical illusion. The
sheer volume of his work means that any particular theme or interest appears slight, however often it
recurred across the decades. And of course the taint of

his English schooling counts against him. As Derek Mahon wrote in his essay 'MacNeice in Ireland and England' (1974): 'The English school system has a way of ironing out regional, and indeed national differences, and turning its products into Englishmen; and this is what happened to MacNeice.' Mahon goes on to observe that his contemporaries were not Patrick Kavanagh or Frank O'Connor, but Auden and Day-Lewis. This is all true enough. But Mahon is on shakier ground when he points out that 'his poetry is of largely English derivation . . . the poets he most admired were Chaucer, Dryden, Keats, Hardy'. To which one might respond: So what? Patrick Kavanagh's place in Irish letters is not threatened by his love of Thomas Gray and Alexander Pope.

Despite the suspicion that MacNeice's Irishness had been neutered by his English education, Mahon conceded that 'some sort of Irish sensibility' permeated his work: 'A mordancy perhaps, and a fascination with the fact of language itself, deriving from an inherited sense of the lethal possibilities of words.'

MacNeice had been dead for over a decade when Mahon wrote those lines, but they would not have surprised him. Such observations on the difficulty of 'placing' MacNeice had a long pedigree and were not always presented in Mahon's fair and insightful fashion. In 1939, MacNeice took part in a radio programme with a man called F. R. Higgins. Higgins was a leading glowworm of the Celtic Twilight who rattled off bad poems about the beauty of abandoned churches and autumn leaves.

MacNeice and Higgins had been asked to discuss 'Tendencies in Modern Poetry.' It quickly became apparent that Higgins had his own agenda in mind. He wanted to talk about why Irish poets—Irish poets not unlike himself—were the best in the world:

> For them the rhythm of their race remains largely unbroken. They are believers, heretical believers, maybe, but they have the spiritual buoyancy of a belief in something... In the Irish poet the racial rhythm is as yet unbroken; while in the young English poet of today the natural rhythm of his race is broken or, even worse, it has ceased altogether to function organically.

If Higgins disliked young English poets, then he had even less time for Americans. T. S. Eliot was nothing but an 'American Victorian', while E. E. Cummings was a charlatan: 'for him poetry is merely a matter of typography.' But his real scorn was reserved for men like MacNeice: 'I don't believe that a poet born in a certain type of society should turn his back on that society...I am afraid, Mr. MacNeice, you, as an Irishman, cannot escape from your blood, nor from our blood-music that brings the racial character to mind.'

All this talk of 'racial rhythm' and 'blood-music' in the summer of 1939 was so obviously fascist in character that MacNeice responded: 'On those premises there is more likelihood of good poetry appearing among the Storm Troopers of Germany than in the cosmopolitan communities of Paris or New York.' To which Higgins replied: 'In some respects I actually believe so'.

Higgins's mystical belief in the purity of Irish blood-music is an interesting footnote in the history of fascist thought, but his conviction that MacNeice was its unwilling heir is more interesting still. MacNeice might be a quisling, but he could not escape from his blood. Afterwards he wrote that 'the man I had the radio discussion with was crazy (he thinks I've sold my birthright)... [and] after denouncing me for 24 hours for having de-Irished myself asked me if I'd like to belong to the Irish Academy of Letters.' Higgins thought MacNeice a traitor, but wanted to give him the opportunity to return to the fold.

MacNeice did not subscribe to the language of racial rhythm and inescapable blood-music, but he might have responded favourably to Mahon's 'inherited sense'. Inheritance was everything. In 1953, when asked to provide a short biography for a speaking engagement, he wrote simply: 'Irish parentage (Gaelic family). Father a Protestant bishop but a nationalist.' Although he lived most of his life in England, he always thought of himself as Irish, a visitor to the English zoo.

When the Second World War broke out, he seemed ambivalent about England's fate. In September 1939 MacNeice reminded a concerned T. S. Eliot that, as an Irish citizen, he was immune from conscription. This attitude was typical of MacNeice, who was not liable to be swept away by jingoistic fervour, however justified. E. R. Dodds remembered him as someone who 'was never prepared to enslave his judgment or his conscience to any "-ism", religious or political; his decisions were his own.' Louis went his own way. But his attitude towards England in 1939 was more than a simple question of personality. It had deep roots:

Even now many Englishmen are unaware of the Irishman's contempt for England.

Although brought up in the Unionist North, I found myself saturated in the belief that the English are an inferior race. Soft, heavy, gullible, and without any sense of humour... In my eyes they were so much foreigners that when the Great War broke out in 1914 (I was then nearly seven) it was some time before I could make out whether it was the English or the Germans who were the enemy.

If the child thought the English inferior, the man found the Irish infuriating. In poetry and prose, he nibbled at the question of Ireland for his entire life. Ireland was not just a place, it was a problem. Northern Ireland was always the focus of his attention and was the source of much of his frustration. The Republic—and particularly the West, home of his forefathers—performed a more romantic role. In his thumbnail biography, 'Irish parentage' is not enough. He goes further and emphasises that his is a 'Gaelic family'. In other words, the real deal. His western origins were always a source of pride, a claim to the 'peasant authenticity' of the kind exemplified by Patrick Kavanagh. It was important that he assert such connections, given that, as he wrote in 'Carrickfergus': 'I was the rector's son, born to the anglican order, / Banned for ever from the candles of the Irish poor.' This predicament occasionally led him to take his western fantasy too far. Despite his privileged upbringing, he wrote that poverty was 'a stratum which is still (instinctively) intelligible to me, my relations are still living in mud-floored cottages in the West of Ireland.' One wonders what Kavanagh would have made of that instinctive intelligibility.

These wistful claims of a western past were all very well, but that was not MacNeice's Ireland. He was a northern man attuned to northern difficulties, albeit from a distance. That distance was vital. He knew Northern Ireland intimately, yet wrote about the place as a learned observer, half-fascinated, half-horrified. At times MacNeice the poet becomes Mac-Neice the character, a character written by Joseph Conrad, some detached emissary from 'civilization' who finds Northern Ireland a dark and alien continent:

> *And how we used to expect, at a later date,*
> *When the wind blew from the west, the noise of*
> *shooting*
> *Starting in the evening at eight*
> *In Belfast in the York Street district;*
> *And the voodoo of the Orange bands*

Drawing an iron net through darkest Ulster,
Flailing the limbo lands—
The linen mills, the long wet grass, the ragged
hawthorn.

              —*Autumn Journal*, XVI

Despite the attachment to his western roots, MacNeice had no patience for misty-eyed blarney in his poetry. His writing on Ireland throughout the 1930s conclusively rejected the twilit dreamland of Æ and Higgins:

The land of scholars and saints:
Scholars and saints my eye, the land of ambush,
Purblind manifestoes, never-ending complaints,
The born martyr and the gallant ninny;
The grocer drunk with the drum,
The land-owner shot in his bed, the angry voices
Piercing the broken fanlight in the slum,
The shawled woman weeping at the garish altar.

              —*Autumn Journal*, XVI

I come from an island, Ireland, a nation
Built upon violence and morose vendettas.
My diehard countrymen, like drayhorses,
Drag their ruin behind them.

Shooting straight in the cause of crooked thinking
Their greed is sugared with pretence of public
spirit.
From all which I am an exile.
                    —'Eclogue from Iceland' (1938)

Reading these poems, I think back to the young William Carleton in Augher, watching the actors attack one another at *The Battle of Aughrim*'s denouement. MacNeice was a poet, but he was a playwright too. His Ireland is an endless drama populated with a cast of complacent characters. Each performs his allotted role, each is fated to declaim his lines and observe his cues at the scripted moment. The actors are keenly aware that they are onstage. Their friends and family are watching them. They must not deviate, they must all carry the play through to its bloody close. As Carleton discovered, the swords they carry are all too real. The final black joke is that the play will run and run. The theatre is leased to the company in perpetuity.

MacNeice did not think much of the play. The violence frustrated and disgusted him: 'It is about time someone kicked that bloody corner of the earth up the arse.' And he was irritated by what he saw as the self-absorption of his fellow countrymen, their belief that Ireland stood at the centre of the universe. This was a phenomenon remarked upon by other Irish writers—George Bernard Shaw wrote that 'Ireland is the Malvolio of the nations, "sick of self-love".' Such assurance clearly amused Shaw, but it enraged MacNeice. He discerned the connection between pathological self-absorption and endless, grinding conflict: 'I hate your grandiose airs, / Your sob-stuff, your laugh and your swagger, / Your assumption that everyone cares / Who is the king of your castle' (*Autumn Journal*, XVI).

MacNeice described himself as an exile from 'violence and morose vendettas.' But he was never exiled from Ireland:

> *Such was my country and I thought I was well*
> *Out of it, educated and domiciled in England,*
> *Though yet her name keeps ringing like a bell*
> *In an under-water belfry.*
>
> —*Autumn Journal*, XVI

> *I can say Ireland is hooey, Ireland is*
> *A gallery of fake tapestries,*
> *But I cannot deny my past to which my self is wed,*
> *The woven figure cannot undo its thread.*
>
> —'Valediction' (1934)

MacNeice visited as often as he could. He championed the work of northern writers like W. R. Rodgers and Patrick Kavanagh. But it is clear that Northern Ireland, although it was his home, was never his world. 'Snow' is a poem about separation and time and the quality of experience. At its core is a wondering revelation:

> *World is crazier and more of it than we think,*
> *Incorrigibly plural. I peel and portion*
> *A tangerine and spit the pips and feel*
> *The drunkenness of things being various.*
>
> —'Snow' (1935)

'Snow' is a poem that communicates a complex and fragile moment: a vase of roses before a window, snow falling outside. The sequence of still roses, transparent glass, and swirling snow provokes a revelation. A vision of plurality. The poem captures a scene that may have passed in a couple of blinks. The portioning out of the tangerine flesh and the 'spawning snow and pink roses against it' are enjoyed for what they are, a brief gasp of sensual delight. No mention is made of Ireland. And yet MacNeice had grown up in a place that was not only plural, but *incorrigibly* so. Such variety, which like roses and

snow remained 'soundlessly collateral and incompat-
ible,' was the essence of his home.

Northern Ireland's inability to reconcile itself to
a reality that was 'incorrigibly plural', to appreciate
'the drunkenness of things being various', was something that Louis MacNeice understood all too well.
In a telling aside, he wrote: 'In Belfast I met a young
man who was wildly anti-everything & spends his
time compiling huge albums of newspaper cuttings.
Museum of human idiocy.' That impatience with
the museum of human idiocy remained with him
always.

*   *   *

The boyhood parallels between C. S. Lewis, Forrest
Reid, and Louis MacNeice are striking. Reading
their memoirs, you often feel that you are hearing
the same story from different lips. Lewis and Mac-
Neice lost their mothers, Reid his beloved Emma and
distant father. All were Protestants, and while some
were more comfortable than others, all were vastly
better off than the average Irishman. All had black
dreams, all became writers. All knew the dark well:
Lewis in the attics of Little Lea, Reid in the flutter-
ing gaslight of the stairwell in 15 Mount Charles,
MacNeice alone in his rectory bed, wondering what

it was that went round the house and waiting for the moment his eyelids would droop, his breath slow, and that same grey monotonous rhythm start up again. Yes, they all knew the dark. But MacNeice knew it best. He carried it with him. Lewis spun his fantasies, Reid found a measure of contentment in his arcadian dreams. MacNeice wrote his sad, exact poems and ended his life where it had begun: in the dark.

> *Afraid of the dark? Come and take light,*
> *Where is your candle? I have no candle,*
> *Only a sword. Which I have not used.*
> —'Cock o' the North' (1950)

In 1963, MacNeice was working on a new radio play, *Persons from Porlock*. The title refers to the man who called on Samuel Taylor Coleridge as he frantically scribbled down 'Kubla Khan' in 1797. The interruption was enough to derail the poem; Coleridge never finished it. MacNeice wrote a play about the interruptions that constantly beset any attempt to create a work of art. Hank, the frustrated artist, is obsessed with caves. MacNeice wanted the play's underground scenes to be as atmospheric as possible. To that end, he accompanied a sound engineer to a cave system in northern England in order to record authentically subterranean drips and moans. After a fruitful day underground, he took a long walk on the moors, where he was drenched in a rainstorm. He travelled back to his home in the south of England that night, still in his wet clothes. Louis MacNeice died of pneumonia three weeks later, on 3 September 1963, at the age of fifty-five. He was cremated and his ashes returned to Northern Ireland. His final resting place is at Carrowdore churchyard, County Down.

MacNeice never stopped writing, but there is no doubt that his finest work was done in the 1930s. The long poem *Autumn Journal* and the collections *Poems* (1935) and *The Earth Compels* (1938) testify to his extraordinary ability. This ability was recognised by other northern writers. A year after MacNeice's death, three young poets gathered at his graveside. Their names were Michael Longley, Derek Mahon, and Seamus Heaney.

CHAPTER SIX

Forked root

Ná luig, ná luig
  fót fora taí:
gairit bía fair,
  fota bía faí.

Take no oath, take no oath
  by the sod you stand upon:
you walk it short while
  but your burial is long.
  —'Ná luig, ná luig', circa eleventh century
                Translated by James Carney

First they have to build the thing. They labour through
June and early July. I never see them working. This is

strange. I walk past the dead ground beside Botanic station several times a day; early in the morning, late at night. But I never see the young men working.

Young men build the fires. Teenagers with marine corps haircuts stack wooden pallets, slotting them together with patience and care, tier after tier, taking direction from older men, as if they were learning how to shave.

Bonfires are going up across Northern Ireland. The young men build them in Donaghadee and Kilcooley and Dundrum. They build them in Augher, Moygashel, Enniskillen, Cullybackey and Castlemara. They build them in Ballykeel and Ballybeen and Ballycraigy and Ballymacash and Ballyduff and Ballycarry and Ballysally and Ballystockart and on Ballywalter beach. There are at least forty pyres under construction in Belfast alone.

Most bonfires are of regulation height and built with approved materials in agreed-upon locations. This is not always the case. On Drumilly Green in Portadown there is a tower 210 pallets high. It is so large that residents of nearby houses are told to board up their windows and leave their homes. In East Belfast a bonfire on the London Road is illegally primed with 1,800 tyres. A ten-minute walk away, pallets have begun to appear in a swimming pool car park.

This is not an approved location for a bonfire, and so contractors are engaged to remove the pallets. They cover their faces for protection, fearful of being identified. Graffiti appears nearby:

MASKED CONTRACTORS—
ATTACK LOYALISM AT YOUR OWN
RISK

The contractors withdraw.

Weeks pass and the bonfire next to Botanic station grows. A strange wedding cake rises over the surrounding streets. The stacked pallets are made from mean planks that swell and blush syrupy orange in the damp. Flags are threaded through them, Union flags for the most part, flags of ownership and defiance. Flags of the barricade.

One July morning the flags have changed and I know that the young men have completed their work. Now that the bonfire is finished, the palette transforms. The red, white, and blue of the United Kingdom are replaced by the green, white, and orange of the Irish Tricolour. Some of these flags are huge. The largest could engulf a double bed. They fill and sag in the breeze and soon they will burn.

They will burn because of a battle fought over

three hundred years ago, on 1 July 1690. The Battle
of the Boyne was fought between James II, King of
England, and William III, King of England. You can
see the problem.

William won. As a child, I imagined that William's victory had been a close-run thing—an outnumbered army, powder burns and broken pikes,
a desperate stand thigh deep in the Boyne's black
water. In fact, William had thirty-six thousand men
under his command, eleven thousand more than
James could muster.

William's army was made up of Englishmen,
Scots, Danes, Dutchmen, Germans, and a liberal
mixture of Huguenots of various nationalities. James
brought French and Irish to the field. William was
born the Prince of Orange, sovereign of the Dutch
Republic. James had spent his youth at the French
court and his adult life in England. The Battle of
the Boyne was a small part of a larger struggle for
the English throne, which was itself an element of a
broader conflict for dominance in Europe. A victory
for James would have benefitted some noble families and destroyed others, but it would have changed
nothing for the overwhelming majority of Irish people. Ireland was a stepping-stone, nothing more.

This is the battle as historians write it. Yet in popular memory, 1 July 1690 remains nothing less than a battle for the soul of Ireland: Catholic James against Protestant William, the old wrestling the new. Today, thanks to the lag introduced by the adoption of the Gregorian calendar, the battle is commemorated on July 12.

All through the evening of July 11, families gather around the bonfires. Despite the sinister circumstances surrounding the construction of some bonfires, this is first and foremost a family event. The shops close early on Botanic Avenue, and women bring out prams and folding chairs. Children are everywhere.

Midnight comes and the fire is lit. Cheap wood burns fast. The pyre next to Botanic station goes up in minutes. The Irish Tricolour thrashes in the warm updraft and vanishes. There is no gout of flame. The flag simply blinks out. Gone.

The crowd sings. Fireworks explode fifty feet above our heads. The people tip their faces as the rockets go up with the sound of tearing cloth. Low detonations and the hiss of flares. Whooping children. The deep roar of the fire behind it all, a fire as large as it will ever be, the people singing still. The party goes on into the small hours. Philip Larkin, who lived in Belfast from 1950 to 1955, described a typical scene in 1951:

> Much more *thrilling* was Sandy Row, the Protestant Quarter, on Wednesday night— bonfires on every street corner blazing up house-high. I strolled down about half past eleven (drizzle coming down as usual) & was fascinated by the cardboard arches across the streets, the thick waves of Guinness, War Horse tobacco, & vinegared chips, the dancing crowds, & the pairs & trios of gum-chewing young girls roaming about wearing paper hats stamped 'No surrender', 'Not an inch', & various Unionist catchwords. Police stood uneasily about in their raincapes.

The enormous scale of today's bonfires is a relatively recent development, but the atmosphere captured by Larkin remains much the same. It is a curious brew. On the one hand, the evening is a family affair. Whole communities come out to watch the pyres go up. Yet there is something else here. The shapes of men cut out of flame. The music and singing. Whoops and shouts in the dark. Thick smoke and the sulphurous reek of fireworks. The whole spectacle tickles a deep region of the human brain. It is increasingly common for pictures of Nationalist politicians to be placed on some bonfires. To burn the image of an enemy is a magical act. Perhaps such magic is as old as our species. It certainly contributes to the atavistic quality of the night. Planes of orange light strike houses and cars, and the light makes these ordinary things foreign.

Northern Ireland is a place absorbed by its own reflection. Much that happens here is a form of mirroring. And so it is no surprise to learn that Catholics once had their own bonfires. These pyres were traditionally lit on August 15 to celebrate the Feast of the Assumption. From 1972, this was superseded by a new date. The religious was supplanted by the political. On 9 August 1971, the Unionist Government introduced a policy of internment without trial in Northern Ireland. Overwhelmed by the scale of the IRA's campaign, the government invoked the Special Powers Act of 1922, which suspended the usual legal thresholds for the arrest and detention of citizens. The first six months saw the arrest of over 2,400 people.

Internment was a shambles from the start. It had been intended to snuff out the growing violence in two key respects. First, the policy would remove paramilitaries from the streets. Second, it would prevent the increasingly outraged Loyalists from taking up arms themselves. Internment failed on both counts.

Large numbers of active paramilitaries were able to evade capture. Many more were not known to the police or army in the first place. To make matters worse, a significant proportion of internees had nothing to do with terrorist activity. Although those found to be innocent were often released promptly, the experience understandably led to the radicalisation of formerly peaceful men. The incompetence of the strategy was matched only by its cruelty. Some detainees received treatment that the European Court of Human Rights described as 'inhuman and degrading'—stress positions, sleep deprivation, white noise. The violence did not subside. It grew. Republicans were enraged. Loyalists, far from being reassured by internment, saw only the increasing chaos that it had produced.

On the evening of 8 August 1972, a new tradition was born. Bonfires were lit to commemorate the anniversary of internment's introduction. Although the policy of internment was ended in 1975, the bonfires burned on August 8 for many years afterwards.

In 2019, the journalist Jake O'Kane described building an August bonfire as a child in North Belfast
during the 1970s. The competition to build the largest bonfire was so intense that rival builders would
poach material from neighbouring pyres: 'More than
once, full-blown riots broke out over such activity,
with befuddled British soldiers looking on, wondering why nationalist youths had begun rioting among
themselves.' O'Kane's recollections echo those of
previous generations. In his autobiographical novel
Reading in the Dark (1996), Seamus Deane recalled the
Derry bonfires of the 1940s:

> Fire was what I loved to hear of and to see. It
> transformed the grey air and streets, excited
> and exciting. When, in mid-August, to com-
> memorate the Feast of the Assumption of Our
> Lady into Heaven, the bonfires were lit at the
> foot of the sloping, parallel streets, against the
> stone wall above the Park, the night sky red-
> dened around the rising furls of black tyre-
> smoke that exploded every so often in high
> soprano bursts of paraffined flame.

Today the Nationalist tradition has found a different form of summertime expression. Féile an Phobail,

a festival of music and culture, is held in West Belfast every August. Féile is a conscious attempt to offer an alternative to tyres and pallets. This is a much slicker affair than the community bonfires it has largely replaced. To the casual observer it looks like any other music festival. Nevertheless, Féile remains a deeply political event. In this respect, it forms an imperfect reflection of the parades that take place throughout Northern Ireland on the Twelfth of July. Imperfect because Féile is static—which is to say, easy to avoid for those who wish to do so—while the parades core through city and country every which way.

You hear the parades well before you see them. This is true when the marching bands are a street away, but it is also true of the weeks leading up to the Twelfth, when the distant bass of practising drummers thrums through early summer. The music is that of an eighteenth-century army advancing in line of battle. Drums that could be heard above the discharge of musket and cannon, bouncing flutes to urge the boys onwards. A veteran of the American War of Independence would feel quite at home.

The sheer volume of the drums is disorienting. At times I have sat in my flat on a July evening and been unable to work out whether the noise is coming from north or south, east or west. The beat and rattle form a clamour that seems to exist everywhere at once. As Seamus Heaney had it in his 'Orange Drums, Tyrone, 1966': 'The air is pounding like a stethoscope.' Yet there is a melancholy to the music. The initial low concussions that build to pure sound before fading away into the night. I think again of MacNeice—'the voodoo of the Orange bands, / Drawing an iron net through darkest Ulster, / Flailing the limbo lands'— and find my own flat made strange to me.

'The limbo lands'. It has always been about the land. Midnight bonfires demonstrate ownership of territory. The parades on the following day—parades that still march to the trill and rattle of the Orange bands—police the boundaries of that territory. The pacing out of the land is an essential annual ritual. We are educated to think of land in terms of acres and miles, but the human step is the only measurement that really matters. This is a fact that is well known to poets here. In 'Land', a poem about taking fleeting ownership of place, Seamus Heaney opens with the lines: 'I stepped it, perch by perch. Unbraiding rushes and grass / I opened my right of way'.

Heaney knew the limbo lands better than anyone. He was born on a farm in County Derry. The farm was called Mossbawn. This was in 1939, but the farmhouse belonged to earlier centuries: 'a one-storey, longish, lowish, thatched and whitewashed house.' Years later, he lovingly mapped his childhood world. The thorn hedge and alder trees that screened Moss- bawn from the road. The beech trees that lined the lane to the house. He picked out the windows and described the kitchen and bedrooms and small sta- ble that lay beyond them. Heaney remembered the cement-floored kitchen with particular affection, a place of constant toil that became a cosy refuge in the evenings. Outbuildings sheltered a few cows, bags of fertilizer, sacks of potatoes, and swallows' nests. His aunt Mary kept a kitchen garden. A succession of horses was used for fieldwork and carting until the tractor replaced them. As a boy, Heaney would lie in bed and listen to the horse in the adjoining stable: 'Big flubby snorts of contentment.'

Most important of all was the pump in the back- yard, the heart of home life. The pump was described by the adult Heaney as the omphalos, a word meaning 'navel'. *Omphalos* was used by the ancient Greeks to indicate the centre of the world, which they believed to be the city of Delphi. Heaney's own *omphalos* was frequented by five families from the surrounding dis- trict for their daily needs.

Mossbawn was no Eden. It was hard work. Though better off than many, the Heaney family still lived 'a subsistence-level life.' And the countryside was seamed with just as many sectarian boundaries as Belfast or Derry:

> The rattle of Orange drums from Aughrim Hill sets the heart alert and watchful as a hare... Like the rabbit pads that loop across grazing, and tunnel the soft growths under ripening corn, the lines of sectarian antagonism and affiliation followed the boundaries of the land. In the names of its fields and townlands, in the mixture of Scots and Irish and English etymologies, this side of the country was redolent of the histories of its owners.

The lines of sectarian antagonism ran through Mossbawn itself. The farm's very name embodied the fractured landscape. Moss-bawn. *Bawn* is a term intimately associated with the Plantation of Ulster.

Hugh O'Neill's rebellion in 1594 had alarmed Elizabeth I and her Privy Council. The House of Tudor lived in constant fear of invasion. Elizabeth's father, Henry VIII, had managed to repulse a vast French invasion fleet at the Battle of the Solent in 1545, but the threat from across the Channel never went away. O'Neill's uprising came just six years after England had been saved from the Spanish Armada by an accident of weather. Ireland was an obvious strategic weakness. A French or Spanish army landed in sympathetic Ireland would be at England's back door, perfectly placed to launch an invasion across the Irish Sea.

The Plantation of Ulster was the Crown's solution to the problem of Ireland. Ulster was viewed as the most fractious of the provinces. The greatest landowners in Ulster had led the uprising of 1594. It made sense to strengthen England's position there. This would be done by seizing huge tracts of the best land and granting the spoils to English and Scottish lords. In return, those lords would ensure that their new properties became home to waves of farmers and artisans from Britain. Ireland's rebellious northeast would be cleared and replanted with Protestants loyal to the English throne. The Tudor regime had experimented with limited plantation schemes by settling Scots and English Protestants in central Ireland as early as 1556. But it was not until 1610, in the wake of Hugh O'Neill's rebellion and subsequent flight, that the Plantation of Ulster began. The English monarch was no longer a Tudor, but the first of its Stuart kings: James I. This first James was the grandfather of James II, who would be defeated by William of Orange at the Battle of the Boyne. By seeding Ulster with Protestants, James I contributed to the demise of his own royal line.

The planters came from many different sections of society. Tracts of northwestern land, including the city of Derry, were granted to the merchant companies of London.* Wealthy English landowners were given large estates of between one thousand and two thousand acres that they were expected to populate with Protestant settlers. Ex-soldiers from the English armies were rewarded with farms and smallholdings. A further 20 per cent of Ulster was reserved for an unexpected category: the 'deserving Irish'. These were native Irish who had helped the Crown defeat O'Neill and who now looked for some reward. Although initially granted good holdings, these deserving Irish were quickly elbowed out of the fertile river valleys. By 1640, most found themselves eking out a living in the hills.

Those Irish lords willing to surrender their lands and titles and swear allegiance to James might be permitted to retain some property and status under the new regime, though they were often disappointed by the results. One Gaelic lord, Conor Roe Maguire, gave his fealty to the Crown only to lose two-thirds of his lands, including his ancestral seat. At the other end of

---

* Hence Derry's seventeenth-century rebranding as 'Londonderry'.

the social scale, the native Irish who were not thought 'deserving' were to be replaced with British farmers and craftsmen. This was easier said than done. As Thomas Bartlett has observed, Irish tenants often outnumbered the British on large estates. They would not be completely replaced until the late seventeenth century.

Settlement was not the only task facing the planters. Ulster was a gift—a gift that they must hold at all costs. The largest estates were expected to build extensive fortifications, while smaller holdings would centre on stone manor houses. Both were to be surrounded by a bawn, a perimeter wall which protected the main dwelling. The word *bawn* is derived from *bábhún* or *badhún*, the Irish term for a cattle enclosure. An Irish word, yet it became synonymous with the high stone walls that were among the most visible reminders of the new dispensation. This was the word—Irish, yet oppressive—which roosted like a cuckoo inside the name of Seamus Heaney's childhood home. The irony was not lost on him: 'So I talked of Mossbawn, / A bogland name . . .'

I'd told how its foundation

Was mutable as sound
And how I could derive

A forked root from that ground,
Make bawn *an English fort,*
A planter's walled-in mound,

Or else find sanctuary
And think of it as Irish,
Persistent if outworn.

—'Belderg' (1975)

Heaney explains his difficulty. To accept *bawn* as a planter stamp, or to cling to its Irish origins, 'outworn' though those origins now were? This was not a difficulty confined to the hedged limits of Mossbawn. It was the problem of Northern Ireland, concentrated into a simple name. Heaney was born eighteen years after the partition of Ireland. He was happy at Mossbawn but knew the place for what it was. A forked root. The past made his longish, lowish house strange. The very name of his birthplace was a root pulled up by his poetry. A root four centuries deep in the black earth.

North (1975), perhaps Heaney's greatest collection, is concerned with forked roots and everything else that the earth conceals. But *North* is also an examination of the earth itself. Heaney takes a childish delight in the physicality of bog, turf, mud, and loam. The ground is a storehouse, a form-giver, a devourer. Bog is an 'Earth-pantry, bone-vault' ('Kinship'), a long-dead woman's nose is 'dark as a turf clod' ('Strange Fruit'), peat is a 'black maw' ('Come to the Bower'). And the earth nurtures too. Antaeus confesses that 'I cannot be weaned / Off the earth's long contour, her river-veins.' The same was true of Heaney.

Most know Heaney for his poem 'Digging' (1966). The heft of his father's spade, his grandfather's deft mastery when cutting turf—this long tradition was closed to Heaney. In 1951, he won a scholarship to St Columb's College in Derry, from which he proceeded to Queen's University Belfast. His first-class degree and subsequent training as a teacher equipped him for a different kind of fieldwork: 'Between my finger and my thumb / The squat pen rests. / I'll dig with it.' The writer becomes earth-turner, archaeologist, even coroner.

Northern Ireland is the result of an argument about land. An argument conducted over four long centuries. Heaney never claimed to understand this place, but he spent a lifetime digging anyway. His poetry is a record of the North's incorrigible plurality, the excavation of a history 'mutable as sound'. Writers have always found a language in the hills, bogs, and glens of this place. C. S. Lewis and Forrest Reid were townies. For them, the countryside was a place to walk and dream. Their land was an inspiration, not an excavation. Leisure rather than work. The Mourne Mountains and Ballycastle beach were places in which they could step sideways into a different world. Despite his yearnings for the Galway of his 'Gaelic family', MacNeice's Ireland was centred on the industrial city of his birth. In 'Belfast' (1931) he wrote: 'Down there at the end of the melancholy lough / Against the lurid sky over the stained water / Where hammers clang murderously on the girders / Like crucifixes the gantries stand.' Yet the bleak architecture of commerce was not his only concern. The land still pulled at him:

> *Among these turf-stacks graze no iron horses*
> *Such as stalk, such as champ in towns and the*
>   *souls of crowds,*
> *Here is no mass-production of neat thoughts*
> *No canvas shrouds for the mind nor any black*
>   *hearses:*
> *The peasant shambles on his boots like hooves*
> *Without thinking at all or wanting to run in*
>   *grooves.*
>
> —'Turf-Stacks' (1932)

Lewis, Reid, and MacNeice responded to the land in their different ways. But none of them got their hands dirty. Heaney did, just as Patrick Kavanagh had done before him. Heaney was always wary when it came to the question of influence. The idea of being 'influenced' by another poet may well have struck him as absurd. A man who had dug up the forked root would naturally be influenced by what had come before. And yet that influence was a complex, amorphous thing. It was not something that could be attributed to any one poet. What mattered was the influence of place and experience. 'Influence' was not a stream, but the seep of water pooling in a bog. It would be a mistake to say that Kavanagh directly influenced Heaney. But the kinship between their work is there for all to see. As he put it: 'Kavanagh walked into my ear like an old-style farmer walking a field.'

Kavanagh had left Inniskeen for Dublin in 1939, the year of Heaney's birth. He came to regret that move. He recognised the Celtic Twilight for what it was, but not before the movement had conscripted him. In 1938, he published an autobiography called *The Green Fool*. This book became his greatest regret. *The Green Fool* detailed his early life, his walk to Dublin, his meeting with Æ, and his first attempts at writing. The facts were all true—or as true as any autobiography ever is—but the mature Kavanagh loathed the tone of his first book. The faux-naive gush of a peasant boy loosed on the world of letters was fundamentally dishonest: 'When, under the evil aegis of the so-called Irish literary movement, I wrote a dreadful stage-Irish, so-called autobiography called *The Green Fool*, the common people of this country gobbled up this stage-Irish lie.'

Kavanagh felt that his best book was *Tarry Flynn* (1948), a novel about a thirty-year-old farmer in a small rural community not unlike Inniskeen. *Tarry Flynn* was honest. It rejected the gilded hokum of *The Green Fool* for the realities of rural life: claustrophobia, stifling religiosity, boredom. Kavanagh looked back on this redemptive novel with characteristic modesty: 'I am humble enough to claim it is not only the best but the only *authentic* account of life as it was lived in Ireland this century (a man shouldn't be afraid to tell the truth even when it is in favour of himself), the principal people who enjoyed this novel were literary sophisticates; its uproarious comedy was too much for the uneducated reader.' Kavanagh may have overestimated *Tarry Flynn*. To describe it as an 'uproarious comedy' seems a bit of a stretch. *Tarry Flynn* is certainly more honest about growing up in the Ulster countryside than *The Green Fool* was, but novel and autobiography shared the same problem: they were books, not poems.

I have lived in important places, times
When great events were decided; who owned
That half a rood of rock, a no-man's land
Surrounded by our pitchfork-armed claims.
I heard the Duffys shouting 'Damn your soul!'
And old McCabe stripped to the waist, seen
Step the plot defying blue cast-steel—
'Here is the march along these iron stones'
That was the year of the Munich bother. Which
Was more important? I inclined
To lose my faith in Ballyrush and Gortin
Till Homer's ghost came whispering to my mind.
He said: I made the Iliad *from such*
A local row. Gods make their own importance.

—'Epic' (1951)

Kavanagh's mature poetry proved fertile ground for Heaney. Not, as we have seen, in the sense that Patrick was a ladder for Seamus to climb. No. Their hands were dirty with the same earth. 'Epic' sees Kavanagh return to the village and the field. It is a recognition that human life is concerned with place and small moments: 'The things that really matter are casual, insignificant little things, things you would be ashamed to talk of publicly. You are ashamed and then after years someone blabs and you find that you are in the secret majority.'

The bellicose farmers of Monaghan are no different to the goatherds and fishermen who set sail for Troy. Both had a poet to witness their 'local row.' And that was enough. In 'Station Island' (1984), Heaney's vision-pilgrimage to the holy island at the centre of Lough Derg, he encounters an unnamed man. He is described as a 'fosterer, / slack-shouldered and clear-eyed.' This fosterer is wry, amused: 'Sure I might have known / once I had made the pad, you'd be after me / sooner or later'. Kavanagh had written his own poem about Lough Derg. He recognised a fellow digger when he saw one.

The best northern writers have always been diggers, though not necessarily with Heaney's conscious intent. In a place where many subjects cannot be approached directly, the land is the preferred metaphor. There is a good reason for this: even in the city, the countryside is never far away. Hills are visible from anywhere in Belfast. Many streets taper away to a wall of hillside. The smell of silage and cow dung still wafts across the city when the wind is right. Pick

a direction, walk for an hour or so, and you will be
surrounded by fields. As Maurice Leitch told me:

> There was the saying, in the early days, if you
> stopped a man in Belfast, every man would
> have seeds in the turnups of his trousers from
> the fields. Because in the early days everybody
> flocked in from the countryside. And that still
> exists to a degree. They never really became
> totally citified. There's always that link with
> the countryside. And relatives, and going to
> the country, and so on... It's a very strange
> milieu. A Victorian linen mill in the heart of
> the green country.

Much nonsense has been written about the northern countryside. Take this strange argument from
E. Estyn Evans: 'In Ulster where you find the drumlins you will hear the drums, for the Protestant planters usually chose the most fertile lowland areas, and I
suspect that people living in such closed-in lowlands
with restricted horizons tend to have a limited vision
and imagination.' Evans is correct in a purely historical sense. The planters did settle the most fertile lowland areas. But his topographical determinism—his
'suspicion' that a life lived on the flat mysteriously

dulls the imagination—is laughable. So is the corol-
lary, that the native Irish forced out into the bogs
and hills are necessarily, as Evans argued, 'poetic and
visionary.' This might seem a compliment at first
glance. In fact, it reduces the Irish to fanciful versi-
fiers trilling gaily down boreen and glen. Nothing
but picturesque faery folk of the kind conjured in
John Hewitt's poem 'Once Alien Here' (1948): 'The
sullen Irish limping to the hills / bore with them the
enchantments and the spells / that in the clans' free
days hung gay and rich / on every twig of every
thorny hedge'.

Evans was wrong. Writers like Ian Cochrane are
proof of that.

Ian Cochrane was born near Cullybackey, County
Antrim, in 1941. Cullybackey is still a small place. It
was even smaller back then. Cochrane was a country
boy, but his land was quite different from Heaney's:
'We lived in a little house right out in the country . . .
seven of us sleeping in one bedroom. But I don't
think I realised we were living in poverty.' There
was no family farm, no horse in the stable. There
was no stable. He wrote six novels. All are mordantly
comic miniatures. All are criminally underread. Patrick Kavanagh would have approved of Cochrane's
work. His plots are the very definition of local rows.

Cochrane was a master of the first sentence. His first novel, *A Streak of Madness* (1973), begins like this: 'The hens were drunk—it was Derek. He got some methylated spirit and soaked bread in it and threw it to them. Then when they started to stagger he went round the yard, killing himself laughing.' Cochrane sustained that note throughout the book. He sustained it throughout his writing life.

He grew up far from the drumlins of County Down. He lived in a world of one-street villages and dying mill towns. His novels are narrated by teenage boys who wander about, grope girls behind hedges, and talk to the old men hanging around on corners. Their families are hollowed out by poverty, drink, and mental illness. The humour is deadpan: 'In other countries people were burnt black with the sun. If you went there they put you in a pot and cooked you alive. In Ireland we were more civilized: we could kill people with guns.'

Humour, but despair too. Cochrane country is a sticky place. Few ever leave. England is somewhere you go to find work and buy fashionable jeans, but you always end up back in the village as if you never went away at all. Industry has arrived—every community centres around its factory or mill—but modernity has not. In *A Streak of Madness*, a schoolteacher and

a faith healer argue over the treatment of a sick boy.
The teacher prescribes Guinness and grape juice. The
faith healer has his Bible.

You might describe Cochrane's characters as outlandish. This would be a mistake. They are true to
life as the young Cochrane lived it. Small Protestant
communities hunkered around church and mill. In *F
for Ferg*, Johnny becomes friends with Fergus, son of
the local factory manager. Fergus lives in a comfortable house and goes to school in England. He is waiting to take up a place at Oxford. He is completely
unprepared for village life:

> 'This is my brother Bill. He's a schizo-
> phrenic,' I say to Fergus. Fergus gave Bill a
> warm handshake.
> 'How interesting,' he says. 'James Joyce
> was a schizophrenic.'
> 'Never heard of him,' Bill says.

No one likes Fergus. He talks about books, not
girls. He is suspected of being a sissy, a 'Norwegian
fruit merchant.' He cannot participate in the sarcasm
and boorishness of the men around him. And yet the
community seduces him: 'There's something very
real about country people.' Page by page, Fergus

becomes part of the furniture, tolerated—though disliked—by people used to the oddness of small places. In the end, it falls to Johnny to push him back out into the wider world.

Cochrane got out too. He went to London in 1959. His sight was bad, and so he spent some time training as a piano tuner. Maurice Leitch was his closest friend, and they roved around London together, drinking and talking. They were known as the odd couple. Leitch tall and lean, Cochrane short and eccentrically dressed: 'sporting long flowing woollen scarves and a tiny child-sized seafaring cap, nimble and neat-footed in his flamenco dancer's shoes.' Leitch visited his London flat often:

It was a one-room flat, it was the living room, and there was the bedroom and the bathroom. It was very dusty because his eyesight wasn't good. And his books were all over the place and he had his typewriter and everything, tapping away. And every afternoon, he would always, if you were out, he would always have to come back to watch *Columbo*. He was obsessed with *Columbo*. He loved *Columbo*. I mean I think Columbo was the sort of person he would feel in touch with, because he only had one eye or something, and that overcoat and the way he talked. But he was obsessed with *Columbo*.

Leitch's novels cover a broader range than Cochrane's work—his most recent, *Gone to Earth* (2019), is set during the Spanish Civil War—but their shared experience of growing up in rural Antrim shone through. Leitch's *The Liberty Lad* (1965) covered much the same territory, though with a more lyrical tone.

Cochrane's literary loves were American. William Faulkner, Flannery O'Connor. The American South was densely settled by Ulster Scots, and Cochrane felt at home among the darkness and absurdity of southern writers. The protagonists in his novels wander about and observe the strange antics of their fellow men, much like Benjy in Faulkner's *The Sound and The Fury*. You wonder about Carson McCullers too—many of Cochrane's characters would not be out of place in *The Ballad of the Sad Café*. Themes of familial disintegration, repressed sexuality, and psychological disability are constants in his work. Cochrane read Faulkner and responded with his own Northern Gothic. His novels are a bridge between two counties: Antrim and Yoknapatawpha. Another forked root unearthed.

* * *

Heaney was one of many young poets, novelists, and playwrights working in Belfast during the 1960s. Michael Longley and Derek Mahon began writing at the same time. The three men went on day trips into the countryside, read one another's work, and engaged in competition that Longley has described as 'combative and no-holds-barred'. They were what R. F. Foster has rightly called 'the great triumvirate of Northern poets', and yet they were the crest of a much broader wave. The playwright Stewart Parker and the novelist Bernard MacLaverty were their contemporaries, along with a host of other gifted young writers. The explosion of talent in Northern Ireland during this period has excited much comment.

Frank Ormsby, who edited several important anthologies of northern poetry, suggested several reasons for Belfast's emergence as a centre of literary creativity during this period. First was the legacy of the 1947 Education Act, which guaranteed free schooling for all children over the age of eleven. This transformed the lives of many children who would not otherwise have been able to complete their educations, particularly in rural Catholic communities, and unlocked much academic potential that might well have gone unrecognised. By the 1960s, the first cohort of the Act's beneficiaries had begun to win scholarships to Queen's University. Heaney acknowledged that his time at Queen's was 'all thanks to the system put in place by that Labour government in Britain.' But access to education was not the whole story. Just as important were new magazines like *Phoenix* and *The Honest Ulsterman*. These journals provided talented young writers with early opportunities for publication, as did the pamphlet series that accompanied the 1965 Queen's University Festival. Ormsby suggested a third and final component to the poetic ferment of '60s Belfast: The Group. This was a writing workshop run by the English poet Philip Hobsbaum, who worked as a lecturer at Queen's. Many of Belfast's most promising writers attended those Monday evenings at Hobsbaum's home, ready to critique and be critiqued. Heaney was a regular, as was Michael Longley. Derek Mahon went once and did not return. It is clear that some found Hobsbaum's salon more useful than others. Heaney valued Hobsbaum's critiques, in particular the suggestion that he should 'roughen up' his poetry. Good advice for a digger.

A fascination with earth, the meat of the land. This is one way to think about Seamus Heaney. There are many others. His career began in earnest with the publication of *Death of a Naturalist* in 1966. He continued to write until his death in 2013. About twelve collections of poetry (depending on how you count them); translations from Irish, Old English, ancient Greek, and Latin; two plays; and a clutch of anthologies and criticism. He taught at Berkeley and Harvard, was professor of poetry at Oxford, and gave innumerable public lectures and interviews. Heaney's range was vast. But his work is unified by a deep moral commitment to his subject. The forked root was to be dug up, wondered at, but never sold.

In 1969, Heaney encountered a book called *The Bog People*, by P. V. Glob: 'The minute I opened it and saw the photographs, and read the text, I knew there was going to be yield from it. I mean, even if there had been no Northern Troubles, no man-killing in the parishes, I would still have felt at home with that 'peat-brown head'—an utterly familiar countryman's face.' These bog people had been preserved in peat bogs for thousands of years. Although

Scandinavia had yielded the largest concentrations of bog burials, some have been found in Ireland too. The National Museum of Ireland in Dublin has bog people on display, low lighting picking out finger-nails and hair.

Many bog people died violent deaths. The Grauballe Man had his throat cut. The Tollund Man was hanged. The Irish bodies displayed in Dublin suffered similar fates. The Old Croghan Man was stabbed in the chest and his body halved after death. Clonycavan Man suffered head trauma and was disembowelled. An Irish poet writing in the 1970s could not help but find a confluence of meanings in these human relics. But if there were parallels to be drawn, there was also respect to be paid.

Heaney was fond of inversion. He enjoyed playing with perspective and expectation, as in 'Lightenings viii' (1991), in which praying monks are transformed into submarine curiosities when a ghostly ship breaches the ceiling of their chapel. Like ghost ships, bog bodies breach the natural order. They refuse to do what dead bodies are supposed to do. Corpses that did not disappear back into the earth, but lingered instead, prisoners of the acidic peat. Heaney's bog people wait. They remember. They even complain: 'My skull hibernated / in the wet nest of my hair. /

Which they robbed. / I was barbered / and stripped /
by a turfcutter's spade' ('Bog Queen', 1975). The bog
queen's resting place beneath the turf is not extraordinary. It is the living above who are the aliens, the
strangers. They come to maim and steal and sell. We
are no longer in the presence of the digger. We listen
to the testimony of the dug-up.

The bog queen, magnificent in peaty gloom, is
rudely awakened: 'I rose from the dark, / hacked bone,
skull ware, / frayed stitches, tufts, / small gleams on
the bank.' To disinter is also to defile. The queen is
deposed, reduced to carefully numbered fragments in
an archaeologist's finds tray. Cleaned and pickled, she
will go on display in a swish museum, her Plexiglas
sarcophagus smudged by the handprints of gawp-
ing tourists. Seamus Heaney knew that digging has
a moral component. Without due care and reverence,
it becomes a kind of sin.

CHAPTER SEVEN

Teethmarks

Light as a skiff, manoeuvrable
yet outmanoeuvred,

I affected epaulettes and a cockade,
wrote a style well-bred and impervious

to the solidarity I angled for,
and played the ancient Roman with a razor.

I was the shouldered oar that ended up
far from the brine and whiff of venture,

like a scratching-post or a crossroads flagpole,
out of my element among small farmers—

I who once wakened to the shouts of men
rising from the bottom of the sea,

men in their shirts mounting through deep
water
when the Atlantic stove our cabin's dead
lights in

and the big fleet split and Ireland dwindled
as we ran before the gale under bare poles.
—'Wolfe Tone', Seamus Heaney (1987)

At 1:56 a.m. on 8 February 1971, a bomb exploded in the heart of Dublin, on the northeast corner of St Stephen's Green. The target was not a police station or a hotel or a pub. The target was a statue.

The statue of Theobald Wolfe Tone had been erected in 1967. It was cast from bronze that eddied between guano grey and the green of beached seaweed. The body seemed almost boneless. His arms were sausages forced awkwardly down the sleeves of a frock coat. Tone's head was too small for his torso and his legs too big. The impression was of a man reflected in unsteady waters.

The incident was not isolated. On 29 October 1969, Tone's grave at Bodenstown, County Kildare, had been bombed by the Ulster Volunteer Force. While no one claimed responsibility for the explosion in St Stephen's Green, it was self-evidently the work of Loyalist paramilitaries. Tone had died in 1798, yet his grave and memorial were considered worthy targets. This was a different kind of warfare, a guerrilla campaign fought not on the streets or in the hills, but in the past.

Theobald Wolfe Tone lived a short life. Born in 1763, dead by 1798. Yet those thirty-five years were enough to cement him as the founding father of Irish Nationalism. The Tones were a family of political firebrands. Wolfe's brother Matthew spent ten months languishing in a French prison on suspicion of espionage. Another brother, Arthur, fought for the United States in the War of 1812. His sister, Mary, spied for France and ended her days in Santo Domingo. Tone went even further. Convinced that it was possible to fulfil Ireland's destiny as a free nation, he went to Paris, where he managed to convince the French to finance a fleet to land an army in Ireland and drive the English out. The 1796 initial invasion failed. Storms prevented the fleet from making landfall at Bantry Bay, and the ships were forced to return to France. A second attempt in 1798 fared even worse. While rebellion against English rule erupted on land, the French fleet was once again unable to reach shore and support them. Gales had scattered the fleet, and Tone's ship, *Hoche*, was surrounded by the Royal Navy. *Hoche* surrendered only once she was all but destroyed: 'with her standing and running rigging all cut to pieces, her masts left tottering, her hull riddled with shot, five feet water in the hold, 25 of her guns dismounted, and a great portion of her crew killed and wounded.' Tone was captured and imprisoned. Found guilty of treason, he was sentenced to hang, but he never reached the scaffold. His death was a murky business. It was officially a suicide, but some whispered murder.

In many respects, Tone was a natural subject for Heaney. He was a crucial figure in Irish history. Had the weather gods been with him, he might well have been able to effect a serious uprising in Ireland. More than that, Tone's journals reveal a deeply sympathetic figure, with an eye for the telling detail. Heaney's line 'men in shirts mounting through deep water' is based on historical fact. The retreat from Bantry Bay in December 1796 was a disaster, the fleet mauled by ever-worsening storms:

December 28. Last night it blew a perfect hurricane. At one this morning a dreadful sea took the ship in the quarter, stove in the other gallery and one of the dead-lights in the great cabin, which was instantly filled with water to the depth of three feet. The cots of the officers were almost all torn down, and themselves and their trunks floated about the cabin. For my part, I had just fallen asleep when waked by the shock, of which I at first did not comprehend the meaning; but, hearing the water distinctly rolling in the cabin beneath me, and two or three of the officers mounting in their shirts, as wet as if they had risen from the bottom of the sea, I concluded instantly that the ship had struck and was filling with water, and that she would sink directly . . . As I knew all notion of saving my life was in vain in such a stormy sea, I took my part instantly, and lay down in my hammock, expecting every instant to go to the bottom.

Tone's obvious talent as a writer, coupled with admirable sangfroid, made him an intriguing subject for a man like Heaney. But there was more to 'Wolfe Tone' than that. By the late 1980s, the Troubles had been raging for over fifteen years. Bloody Sunday on 30 January 1972, Bloody Friday on 21 July 1972, the

Birmingham pub bombings on 21 November 1974, the La Mon restaurant bombing on 17 February 1978, the Enniskillen Remembrance Day bombing on 8 November 1987. These were among the worst atrocities. But there was the day-to-day nature of the Troubles too. The checkpoints, the suspicion, the numbers of civilian dead slowly mounting with every passing week.

Heaney felt the weight. All serious northern writers did. Northern Ireland was a place in which words could kill. A careless phrase, a flashy headline, an unqualified statement, even a stupid joke— all these things were dangerous. Language was used rashly during the Troubles. Careless words deepened division with every passing day. This carelessness might take the form of Ian Paisley's venomous rants. Equally, it might be the casual dismissal of someone as a Fenian or an Orange Bastard or a Tan.* While speech was often used with reckless abandon between communities, it was rigorously policed within them. Informers—'touts'—were dealt with swiftly.

---

* A pejorative term for English people, still widely used today. A reference to the Black and Tans, the militarized police force largely composed of British ex-soldiers, that inflicted enormous suffering on the Irish populace between 1920 and 1922.

Language was a weapon, and was therefore a tool of control as well.

This was the context in which Heaney found himself. To write about the Troubles was like walking through a powder magazine with a lit candle. Every step must be taken carefully, the flame guarded with a cupped hand. Glibness, carelessness. These were the real enemies. In 'Whatever You Say, Say Nothing' (1975), Heaney describes the journalistic machine that descended on Northern Ireland in the 1970s:

> *Where media-men and stringers sniff and point,*
> *Where zoom lenses, recorders and coiled leads*
> *Litter the hotels. The times are out of joint*
> *But I incline as much to rosary beads*
>
> *As to the jottings and analyses*
> *Of politicians and newspapermen*
> *Who've scribbled down the long campaign from gas*
> *And protest to gelignite and sten*

A tragedy measured in column inches. A tragedy *fed by* column inches. Reportage hungry for the gory detail and the front-page photograph. Three explosions for the two-minute bulletin. Wide shot of the bombed-out street. An interview with the bereaved.

The responsible poet had to avoid such voyeurism at
all costs. Perhaps it was better not to write at all. You
never knew what you might dig up. But what were
you left with, then? Only the bewildered speech of a
people grown used to automatic platitudes:

> *Expertly civil-tongued with civil neighbours*
> *On the high-wires of first wireless reports,*
> *Sucking the fake taste, the stony flavours*
> *Of those sanctioned, old, elaborate retorts:*

> *'Oh, it's disgraceful, surely, I agree.'*
> *'Where's it going to end?' 'It's getting worse.'*
> *'They're murderers.' 'Internment,*
> *   understandably . . .'*
> *The 'voice of sanity' is getting hoarse.*

The poem takes its title from the lines 'Where
to be saved you only must save face / And whatever
you say, say nothing.' But the real punch comes two
stanzas earlier, with the exclamation

> *Christ, it's near time that some small leak was*
> *   sprung*

> *In the great dykes the Dutchman made*

To dam the dangerous tide that followed Seamus.
Yet for all this art and sedentary trade
I am incapable . . .

A small leak. Heaney sings of a dam, but he might as well have described a trepanning, a small hole drilled into the skull to relieve pressure that would kill were it allowed to build and build. 'Christ, it's near time'. He feels himself unequal to the task. His genius cannot find a purchase on the skull, the dam is too strong. The right tone is elusive, and until he has found it, he is silenced. Yet he has a duty to speak. Not for himself, but for those ordinary people who are trapped in a world gone mad:

Where half of us, as in a wooden horse
Were cabin'd and confined like wily Greeks,
Besieged within the siege, whispering morse.

Macbeth act 3, scene 4 finds the king of Scots complaining that once he was 'Whole as the marble, founded as the rock, / As broad and general as the casing air: / But now I am cabin'd, cribb'd, confined'. Macbeth's only release is death. Heaney, by grafting Shakespeare onto Homer, offers an imperfect alternative. Wily Odysseus captures Troy with his wooden horse, but he is then consigned to a decade adrift, hopping from one strange island to another as he searches for his home.

Confinement is a recurring theme in the literature that has come out of the Troubles. The most developed example of this social imprisonment was published relatively recently. *Milkman* won the Booker Prize in 2018. The author, Anna Burns, was born in Belfast in 1962. She grew up in Ardoyne, a Catholic area of north Belfast which was a centre of Republican paramilitary activity during the Troubles.

There is only one real name in *Milkman*. Every other character is given a designation instead: 'maybe-boyfriend', 'Somebody McSomebody', 'middle-youngest sister'. The teenage narrator is middle sister. The city is never named, and neither are the two enemies, 'the other religion' and 'the state'. Middle sister lives in her small part of the city in the late 1970s. Her neighbourhood is run by paramilitaries. Social norms are enforced with violence and with gossip. When middle sister attracts the interest of a notorious paramilitary known as the Milkman, she becomes a victim of both. Burns tells the story of a young woman cabin'd by war and her own community. Surveillance is constant. Everyone watches everyone else. The 'rules of allegiance' are endless:

There was food and drink. The right butter. The wrong butter. The tea of allegiance.
The tea of betrayal. There were 'our shops'
and 'their shops.' Placenames. What school
you went to. What prayers you said. What
hymns you sang. How you pronounced your
'haitch' or 'aitch.' Where you went to work.
And of course there were bus stops. There was
the fact that you created a political statement
everywhere you went, and with everything
you did, even if you didn't want to.

There is a constant suspicion that everyone is up
to something. When a group of feminists try to hire
a small hut as a venue for their meetings, there is an
outcry from the local area. Feminists are beyond the
pale, and their attempt to rent a hut is regarded as
deeply sinister: 'They could be up to anything in it.
They could be having homosexual intercourse in it.
They could be performing and undergoing abortions
in it.'

Middle sister is already regarded by the
community—including her own family—as a suspicious character. She reads books while walking along the street, an eccentricity that marks her
out as 'one of those intemperate, socially-outlawed

beyond-the-pales.' She rejects the advances of Somebody McSomebody, who sends her melodramatic
love letters: 'In it he'd threatened to kill himself in
our front garden only we didn't have a garden. In
a second letter, this was amended to "outside your
front door." ' When the Milkman begins to stalk her,
the community assumes that this is because middle
sister is sleeping with him.

Burns finds comedy in this hothouse atmosphere.
Despite the details of the plot, *Milkman* is a very
funny book. But beneath the humour lies the grim
reality lived by so many ordinary people during the
Troubles. The stifling claustrophobia of a small community tormented by paramilitaries within and the
state without, 'besieged within the siege'.

Heaney, Burns, and thousands of others found
themselves on their own strange island. There was no
escape. Unlike Odysseus, they were already home.
Yet still they drifted. Heaney's task was to find an
anchor. An outlet for his 'sedentary trade'. To explain
his own home to himself. The past allowed him to do
this with care, nuance, and respect.

The past offered the safety of distance. Its anach-
ronistic grammar allowed a different mode of speech.
Wolfe Tone could be dug up and displayed. His body,
his life, became the vehicle for an oblique commentary

on the present. 'Wolfe Tone' is from *The Haw Lantern* (1987), Heaney's most enigmatic collection. The poems are probing and doubtful. Tone is delivered from drowning in the darkness of the great cabin only to be confined in a dark cell a few years later. Hope dies. 'The Disappearing Island' is also from *The Haw Lantern*. Tone's foiled dreams are echoed in the islanders' failed attempt to build a home. Just as the thwarted revolutionary watches Ireland dwindle behind his ship, the islander remembers the dreadful moment when 'the island broke beneath us like a wave.' Both despair at the wreck of their hopes. Both are undone by water. Man's solid plans dissolve: 'Now it's high watermark / And floodtide in the heart / And time to go' ('Voices from Lemnos', 1990).

Writing about the Troubles was a moral act. An oblique approach was a response to that duty of care and nuance. But there was a further concern. In a time when ordinary men, women, and children were being killed as they went about their daily lives, what good was writing at all?

'Chekhov on Sakhalin' (1984) is another poem centred on an historical figure. Anton Chekhov (1860–1904) is best known as a playwright and master of the short story, but he was also a medical doctor. In 1890, he made the long journey from Moscow to Sakhalin Island, a Russian possession to the north of Japan. Sakhalin was a penal colony. Chekhov wanted to write a scientific study of the conditions there, 'and thus to repay a little the science of medicine.' In Heaney's poem, Chekhov is troubled by the spectacle of chained men, appalled by this island of half-starved prisoners. His own freedom haunts him. He wonders how he will write his book: 'To try for the right tone—not tract, not thesis—/ And walk away from floggings.' Heaney spent his life searching for the right tone. Like Chekhov, perhaps he saw in himself the entirely natural impulse to walk away from floggings. To see unbridled, purposeless cruelty and know that nothing was to be done. And to wonder if an act of witness would change anything at all.

Sakhalin was another island with a dark heart. A natural addition to Heaney's archipelago. But there were other zones of interest too. Chekhov did write a book about his experiences on the island, *Sakhalin Island* (1895). Although I suspect Heaney based his poem on Chekhov's letters alone, there was much in *Sakhalin Island* to pique his interest. The population of Alexandrovsk 'live, like the Irish, on nothing but potatoes.' And the book contains an episode that might well have resonated with a poet who was uncertain about writing in the face of violence.

Chekhov's compulsive note taking gave rise to complaints among the prisoners: 'Write, write, bloody write, that's all they ever do, God 'elp us!'

Heaney composed 'Chekhov on Sakhalin' during the Hunger Strikes of 1980–1981, when IRA men held at the Maze Prison outside Belfast refused food in protest at their treatment as criminals as opposed to political prisoners. Just as Chekhov turned away from the flogging and was ashamed, Heaney felt what he described as 'self-accusation': 'If I had followed the logic of the Chekhov poem, I'd have gone to the prison, seen what was happening to the people on the hunger strike and written an account of it, "not tract, not thesis".' He wrote a poem instead, because that was all he could do—open a small leak in the dam. Others followed his example.

In February 2020 I went to see a small exhibition at the Bank of Ireland in Dublin.

The exhibition was called *Seamus Heaney: Listen Now Again.* A series of small galleries held a selection of relics. I thought of the bog people who lie in the National Museum of Ireland, no more than a ten-minute walk away. Drafts of poems, a blackthorn stick. Heaney's desk, which consisted of two planks of wood balanced on filing cabinets. The most moving item on display was a letter written by Heaney to

a young man from County Armagh. The seventeen-
year-old had sent Heaney some poems and asked to
be told where he was going wrong. Heaney replied:
'I like these poems very much and I think you don't
need anyone to tell you "where you're going wrong."
I think you're a poet and will go where you decide.'
The young poet was called Paul Muldoon.

Muldoon was born in Portadown, County
Armagh, in 1951. His first collection of poems (*New
Weather*, 1973) was published while he was still a student at Queen's University Belfast. In 2003, he won
the Pulitzer Prize for Poetry. His poetry is sly, often
funny. *Quoof* (1983) is 'our family word / for hot
water bottle,' and Muldoon laughs at the way he has
spread this unique domestic slang across the world in
his wake: 'I have taken it into so many lovely heads'.
Words are like honey on fingers. Sticky, spreadable.
Even erotic. In 'Whim' (1980), a man spots a girl
reading Irish legends in Belfast's Europa Hotel. Ireland's mythological past is an opportunity for flirtation. The girl is reading an outdated translation from
the Irish, and the man is only too happy to advise her
on something better:

> He smiled. She was smiling too.
> 'If you want the flavour of the original

You should be looking to Kuno Meyer.
As it happens, I've got the very edition
That includes this particular tale.
You could have it on loan, if you like,
If you'd like to call back to my place, now.'

The geeky come-on works a charm. They go to
the Botanic Gardens, and the tone changes. Cheeky
flirtation over Irish mythology shifts into something
stranger. Lovemaking in the shrubbery, and then a
'Full stop':

They lay there quietly until dusk
When an attendant found them out.
He called an ambulance, and gently but firmly
They were manhandled onto a stretcher
Like the last of an endangered species.

We are left to guess what that species might be.
No guesswork is required for 'Meeting the British'
(1987), a history poem in which Muldoon dug up the
French and Indian War.

American parallels with Northern Ireland offer
a particularly rich historical avenue for poets and
novelists. The Colony of Virginia was chartered in
1606 and settled in 1607, the same decade in which

the Plantation of Ulster began in earnest. Muldoon's interest lies over a century later, and much farther north—the British are met in what is now Canada. This encounter between an indigenous people and foreign invaders occurs in midwinter, within earshot of 'the sound of two streams coming together / (both were frozen over).' The two streams meet, but only as unyielding ice. There can be no mixing of waters until the distant thaw. The poem's narrator will never see that thaw. He accepts a gift from the British that will spell the end of his way of life: 'They gave us six fishhooks / and two blankets embroidered with smallpox.'

Brian Moore explored similar territory in his novel *Black Robe* (1985). Moore was born in Belfast in 1921 and emigrated to Canada in 1948. His Belfast childhood, coupled with his adult life in Montréal, resulted in a great historical novel. Father Laforgue, a Jesuit priest, travels by canoe from Québec City to take up his post at a mission in Huron territory. The Algonquin, Iroquois, and Huron he encounters on his journey call him the Blackrobe. Moore did not intend his novel to be an allegory for Northern Ireland. But he admitted that subconscious forces may have been at play when he wrote it: 'The only thing they have in common is the view that the other side must be the Devil. If you don't believe in the Devil, then you can't hate your enemy and that may be one of the most sinister things about Belfast today.' When Blackrobe encounters an Innu hunchback, he is accused of being a demon:

> Laforgue felt himself start. 'Why do you say that?' he asked.
>
> 'Because *I* am a demon,' the hunchback said. 'Oh yes, everyone knows it. I entered the cunt of an Algonkian woman thirty winters past and was borne by her as a child. And you, Blackrobe, you also are a demon.'

The hunchback sees a demon in the robed European. And the European sees a devil in the hunchback:

> A sorcerer. Laforgue thought of what Father Brabant had written in the *Relations*: 'The sorcerers are our greatest enemies...I fear that they may traffic with the devil.'

Moore describes two men who cannot understand one another. Their response is to believe that their fellow man is a demon, an instrument of evil.

Muldoon's poem is even darker. The Indigenous narrator of 'Meeting the British' opens himself to the possibility of friendship. As a result, he loses everything: a life, a land, a culture. It is an act of communication, the acceptance of a gift, that kills. Dialogue brings its own dangers.

Heaney, Muldoon, and Moore found that the past offered a kind of solution to the difficulty of writing about the Troubles. Other oblique approaches proved just as useful.

Medbh McGuckian was born in Belfast in 1950. Critics have often drawn parallels between McGuckian and other female Irish poets of her generation. She resisted the comparison. Eavan Boland and Nuala Ní Dhomhnaill were her contemporaries, but they were from the South. Boland grew up in England and Dublin, Ní Dhomhnaill in West Cork and County Tipperary. Their poetry was written under different skies. Experience and place formed connective tissue, not sex: 'The poets from the South haven't had this experience of not being free to walk down the street or of having a gun pointed at you, which Heaney had and Paul Muldoon has. So I feel more connected to them as poets than any woman from the South who has never experienced that.'

McGuckian's poetry has a reputation for difficulty.

Perhaps this is because her work places such emphasis on tone. Images are carefully selected, and these vivid word-pictures overlap on the page, collage rather than narrative. Like a painting, a McGuckian poem can be taken in whole. In a 2005 interview, she described the sadness that she discerned:

> Floating in the trees and in the mountains and in the clouds, floating around, less concentrated but something similar, to me, a great sadness. I always thought this sadness was within me, but gradually I understood that everything that was happening now was because of something that had happened then.

McGuckian experiences a great sadness in Ireland's landscape. The reader finds a similar diffuse melancholy in her poetry. Much of her work—perhaps all of it—addresses the Troubles in one way or another. McGuckian wrote 'Drawing Ballerinas' (2001) in memory of her friend Ann Frances Owens, one of two women killed on 4 March 1972, when a bomb exploded in the Abercorn Restaurant in central Belfast. The title is taken from Henri Matisse, who said that he had endured the Second World War by drawing ballerinas.

The body turns in, restless, on itself, in
a womb of sleep, an image of isolated sleep.
It turns over, reveals opposing versions of itself,
one arm broken abruptly at elbow and wrist,
the other wrenched downwards by the force of the
*   turning.*

It settles under its own weight, like some weighty
nude. It flattens to the surface on which it lies,
a series of fluid, looping rhythms, let loose
by one last feeling . . .

It is possible to pick these lines apart, to dig up
the body at the centre of this poem. But it is better
just to sit with it. To permit the images to expand
and contract as you read and reread, and allow the
diffuse sadness to do its work. 'Drawing Ballerinas'
is powerful precisely because of what it does not say.
McGuckian's sidelong, angled approach is one of the
best examples of poetry that addresses the horrors
of the Troubles without stooping to detailed vulgarity. This was the approach favoured by most writers
of the time. Indeed, the finest poem written about
the Troubles was composed in just such a sidelong
register: 'A Disused Shed in Co. Wexford' by Derek
Mahon.

Mahon was born in 1941. He grew up in Belfast and attended Trinity College Dublin and the Sorbonne. He began writing poetry as a schoolboy, and in Christmas 1958 he won the Forrest Reid Memorial Prize for a poem called 'The power that gives the waters breath.' Mahon was educated at the Royal Belfast Academical Institution, the same school that Forrest Reid attended, and a prize had been founded in honour of Belfast's leading Edwardian novelist. Forty-seven years after he had won the award, Mahon published *Harbour Lights* (2005), a collection that includes the short poem 'A Garden God':

A bomber fly flits from the ruined mouth;
from the eye socket an inquisitive moth.

This is not considered one of Mahon's major works. It has been described as a pagan tableau, 'a brief two-line *memento-mori* focused on a weathered statue.' The title's similarity to Reid's second novel, *The Garden God*, may simply be a coincidence. Whether or not Mahon intended some tip of the hat to a fellow alumnus, the comparison between novel and poem is a fruitful one. The two writers began from the same image and arrived at very different conclusions. Where Reid found youth and beauty,

Mahon diagnosed decay. An odd slump at the bottom of the garden, a grisly intrusion, just as the reader intrudes to scare fly and moth away. Dark pooled in Mahon's poetry.

Mahon never achieved Heaney's global recognition. But he was recognised, along with Michael Longley, as one of the three great poets who came of age in 1970s Northern Ireland. Most of his adult life was spent away from Belfast—he lived in Dublin and London before finally settling in Kinsale, County Cork. Like Heaney, the young Mahon wondered what use he was in the face of meaningless violence. He too was consumed by self-accusation:

> *What middle-class shits we are*
> *To imagine for one second*
> *That our privileged ideals*
> *Are divine wisdom, and the dim*
> *Forms that kneel at noon*
> *In the city not ourselves.*
>
> —'Afterlives' (1975)

Much of the work chosen for Mahon's *Selected Poems* is marbled with classical imagery. Mahon was hardly alone in this preoccupation with Greece and Rome. Seamus Heaney adapted Sophocles. Louis

MacNeice and Michael Longley were both trained classicists. Yet Mahon's ancient world is the one that lives for me, perhaps because those long-ago names seem unforced in his mouth. Mahon is a poet of dawn and dusk—I cannot imagine reading him at two o'clock in the afternoon—and his poems are a natural home for the abandoned, built-over, and forgotten.

Mahon never used antiquity as wallpaper. This is not the classical past. It is the classical passing by our noses. Palinurus, Heraclitus, Tacitus. Rome and Alexandria. The isles of Paros, Naxos, and Ithaca: baskets of lemons carried back across the Irish Sea. Pompeii is excavated time and again by Northern Irish writers, and Mahon was no exception:

> *Driving west in the evening from Pompeii,*
> *its little houses sealed up in a tomb*
> *of ash and pumice centuries ago*
> *and now exposed to the clear light of day . . .*
> —'Ghosts' (2011)

Pompeii, its shop fronts gaudy in ochre and red, its temples and brothels and taverns, its peristyled gardens offering respite from merchants and oxen, has moved writers since the first hours of Vesuvius's eruption. The city's very name is a gift: hearty *Pom* saddened by fading *peii*. Ruined homes and the casts of the dead had an uncanny resonance for someone who had experienced the Troubles, even at a distance: 'And I step ashore in a fine rain / To a city so changed / By five years of war / I scarcely recognize / The places I grew up in' ('Afterlives').

Mahon's masterpiece was set closer to home, though still at a remove from Northern Ireland. 'A Disused Shed in Co. Wexford' (1975) hangs on a simple act. Someone opens the door of an abandoned shed to discover that it has become home to a vast colony of mushrooms: 'A thousand mushrooms crowd to a keyhole. / This is the one star in their firmament / Or frames a star within a star. / What should they do there but desire?' The visitor takes a photograph of this unsettling fungal landscape. There is the horror of discovery. The shock of life. Again we find the confinement of Heaney's wooden horse and Burns's nameless city. And again, the silence is total. This unexpected colony says nothing: 'They have learnt patience and silence / Listening to the rooks querulous in the high wood.'

There have been deaths, the pale flesh flaking
Into the earth that nourished it;

And nightmares, born of these and the grim
Dominion of stale air and rank moisture . . .

They have been waiting such a long time: 'in a foetor / Of vegetable sweat since civil war days'. No one cares for them. No one even knows that they exist. Those outside in the sunlight think nothing of the disused shed itself, let alone the life it cabins and confines. Prison and prisoner are equally overlooked.

They are begging us, you see, in their wordless
 way,
To do something, to speak on their behalf
Or at least not to close the door again.
Lost people of Treblinka and Pompeii!
'Save us, save us,' they seem to say,
'Let the god not abandon us
Who have come so far in darkness and in pain.
We too had our lives to live.
You with your light meter and relaxed itinerary,
Let not our naive labours have been in vain!'

The final stanza is a retreat of sorts. A retreat from the oblique and allegorical. The door swings open. Harsh light pours in on suffering and dismay. Many have already given up, waited too long: 'For their deliverance, have been so long / Expectant that there is left only the posture.' Those that remain vital wish only to be spoken for, or at the very least, not forgotten again. Mahon's poem cannot save them. But it leaves the door ajar.

The Troubles posed questions of enormous difficulty for the writers who lived through them. Heaney and Mahon moved away from Northern Ireland, and perhaps that redoubled their need to find the right tone. To speak the truth without exploiting the tragedy as it unfolded day by day. This was not a literary problem. It was a moral imperative. 'A Disused Shed in Co. Wexford' is the finest example of a poetry that sought to address an entire society imprisoned by violence and fear. But there were some injustices that required a more targeted response. One such tragedy was addressed by Michael Longley with his poem 'Kindertotenlieder'.

Michael Longley was born in Belfast in 1939 to English parents. He studied classics at Trinity College Dublin, though he spent most of his time writing poems and indulging his passion for jazz and rugby—while still an undergraduate, he referred to himself as a 'lapsed classicist'. He became close friends with Derek Mahon at Trinity, and lived with him in a grim basement flat on Merrion Square after graduation.

He did not meet Seamus Heaney until his return to Belfast in 1963. Longley attended Hobsbaum's Group, a workshop he has since described as 'over-mythologised.' Of the three men, Longley was the only one to remain in Northern Ireland throughout the Troubles. This proximity meant that the difficulty of writing—or not writing—about the violence in the North was perhaps particularly acute for him. A series of poems about World War One allowed him to address violent death at a remove from the immediate Irish context. Yet some of the events happening around him in Belfast were so appalling that they required a different approach. 'Kindertotenlieder' is just such a poem.

The three Shorland armoured cars were manufactured by Short Brothers of Belfast. The men who crewed them were officers of the Royal Ulster Constabulary, and the streets they patrolled were ostensibly British streets. Only the machine guns were foreign. They had been designed by John Browning of Ogden, Utah, a celebrated gunsmith and enthusiastic polygamist. The first Browning machine guns were intended for use on the battlefields of the Western Front. On the evening of 14 August 1969, a policeman used one to strafe a block of flats in West Belfast, and a nine-year-old boy died.

The names of the policemen involved that night were hidden. During the subsequent enquiry, they were cyphered as Mr X, Mr V, Mr U, and Mr Y. These cyphers couldn't agree on much. The locals were rioting. Petrol bombs were flying. The three armoured cars drove along a section of Divis Street. Shots were fired from inside St Comgall's, the local primary school. Automatic fire, Mr X said, not some chancer having a crack with an antique rabbit gun. Mr X ordered his gunner to give the school a few rounds 'for effect'. The gunner obliged with three bursts from his Browning.

A makeshift barricade had been thrown up across Divis Street. The Shorlands crushed it and turned around. As they passed St Comgall's for the second time, Mr U reported seeing a man standing outside a block of flats nearby. This man threw a 'silvery object' beneath Mr U's Shorland. A detonation rocked the vehicle. Mr U ordered his gunner to fire on the man as he ran away. His gunner, Mr Y, was adamant that this burst from his Browning did not hit the block of flats.

In flat number 5, a boy called Patrick Rooney was getting ready for bed. The street was ablaze, the air one great howl, and still a nine-year-old boy was going about his business, brushing his teeth, undressing, pulling back his sheets. When the shooting intensified, Patrick's father decided to gather his family in the flat's rear. Neely Rooney picked up his son and carried him into another room. There the Rooneys waited as the gunfire intensified.

Later, Neely Rooney would not describe what he heard, though the noise must have been deafening. He spoke only of what he saw. Weird flashes in the room, and his son on the floor. Neely's forehead had been clipped by a bullet. The family thought that Patrick had fainted at the sight of his father's blood. Patrick Rooney had not fainted. He had been shot in the back of the head.

Eyewitnesses describe the Shorland cars unloading their Brownings into the flats. Forensic evidence backs them up. The tracks of four bullets were found in flat number 5, and ballistics experts concluded that these had been created by a high-velocity armament discharged from a position six to eight feet above ground level—as if this powerful weapon had been mounted on a vehicle. An armoured car, say.

Flat number 5 was not alone. A further twelve flats in the same complex were strafed by gunfire, much of it high-velocity rounds of the type that killed Patrick Rooney. All of the Shorland crews denied shooting at the flats.

The head of the inquiry, Lord Justice Scarman, concluded:

The Shorland crew members offer no explanation for the high-velocity bullet damage done
to the central area of the flats. If they are to
be believed, this was not caused by Shorland
fire: but we find that it was. The ballistic
evidence, and the testimony of civilian wit-
nesses, put the fact of Shorland shooting into
the central area of the flats beyond doubt.

Scarman was convinced that the Shorland crews
had lied about their actions that night. One of those
police officers had killed a child.

The inquiry into the events of 14 August 1969
was published between sky-blue covers as the 'Scarman Report', properly entitled *Violence and Civil Disturbances in Northern Ireland in 1969*. The report dealt
with the death of Patrick Rooney and many others caught in the crossfire. It is an exemplar of legal
English. Qualifications and subclauses unspool across
numbered paragraphs. Conflicting testimonies are
compared, independent experts consulted. This is one
way to write about the murder of a child. The horror is dissected, parsed, organised. Dispassion dem-
onstrates competence. Lawyers have it easy. Lawyers
can hide behind their work, just as Rooney's killer hid
behind a letter of the alphabet.

Michael Longley could not hide. If a poet could not write about Patrick Rooney, then what was poetry for? Yet, as Longley wrote in 2014:

> From the outset it has been (and still is) hugely difficult—impossible even—to find in poetry a voice, as Seamus Heaney put it, "adequate to our predicament"... We took our time. Paul Muldoon observed that if you didn't write about the Troubles you might be dismissed as an ostrich; if you did, you might be judged exploitative.

Michael Longley had to write an impossible poem. So he got to work:

> *There can be no songs for dead children*
> *Near the crazy circle of explosions,*
> *The splintering tangent of the ricochet,*
>
> *No songs for the children who have become*
> *My unrestricted tenants, fingerprints*
> *Everywhere, teethmarks on this and that.*

No songs: Longley admits his difficulty early. To name Patrick Rooney would be invasive, even exploitative. So he doesn't write about Patrick, about dead children. He writes about what they leave behind. First the circles and tangents, cruel geometry of violence. Next, the innocent shades, squatting in the poet's mind. Fingerprints, yes, and they are everywhere, traces of holding, playing, of being in the world. But there are also teethmarks. Biting now, a clenched jaw, anger or pain, a final image of desperate violence as the poem closes.

Longley named his poem 'Kindertotenlieder' ('Songs for Dead Children'), after a song cycle composed in 1904 by Gustav Mahler. Mahler in turn had based his work on a collection of poems written by Friedrich Rückert. The title is apt in an obvious way, part of the laboured game of winking reference that Europe's poets have played for two thousand years or more. But it serves a deeper purpose. German snarls the poem's beginning, trips the reader, offers a diversion from immediate Troubles and points down the bleak track of the twentieth century. Longley is not writing a song for the dead children of Northern Ireland. There can be no such songs, after all. He opens his poem up and sings of the ghostly marks that all children, everywhere, leave when they are gone—including Patrick Rooney.

CHAPTER EIGHT

The Strangers' House

Ireland is a small place geographically, and even smaller socially. This is doubly true of the North. The writers who came of age in the 1960s knew one another, drank together, appeared in the same anthologies and magazines. They were faced with the same range of problems, particularly the difficulty of responding to the Troubles in a way that was both sensitive and truthful. While their relationship to literary forebears was often complex, it was always acknowledged. When Seamus Heaney, Derek Mahon, and Michael Longley visited the grave of Louis MacNeice in 1964, they paid tribute to a poet who exemplified the problem of Northernness. MacNeice found his birthplace both fascinating

and exasperating. An Irishman in London, yet criti-
cised by men like F. R. Higgins for not being Irish
enough. A man who celebrated his Western ancestors
despite his comfortable childhood in a Carrickfergus
rectory. A Protestant with Nationalist sympathies.
Naturally, these were not the precise problems faced
by Heaney, Mahon, and Longley. But they were
quintessentially *northern* problems. Problems that
prompt questions about home and history that must
be explored by any northerner serious about unpick-
ing the complexities of their birthplace.

The great attraction of tribalism in Northern Ireland is that such questions do not need to be asked.
Prior generations have already provided the answers.
The story—Unionist or Nationalist—has been tested
and refined over the centuries. Difficulties are dismissed, hypocrisies omitted, history simplified and
artfully rearranged. Above all, challenges are antici-
pated. This is why even the most animated political
debates, whether they are conducted at the highest
levels of government or in a sticky-floored pub, have a
stale and disingenuous quality. Grievance and counter-
grievance. Fact and counterfact. The purpose of such
debates is not to persuade the opposition that they are
in the wrong about a given issue. It is to bolster one's
own tribal story. Mythology is born of repetition.

A tribal writer will never produce great work. In the hundred years of Northern Ireland's existence, there has not been a single poet or novelist of any worth who has succumbed to the cosy certainties of the tribe. The best northern writers have rejected the answers that their respective communities offer up. Perhaps this is the root of the homesick quality that, for me, defines Northern Irish writing. It is difficult to exchange certainty for doubt, and lonely too.

This book began with Tom Paulin's poem 'An Ulster Unionist Walks the Streets of London'. The Unionist discovers that he is not at home but abroad. He is shaken by the discovery of his own foreignness and is spurred into action. The death of certainty terrifies him. He must begin to ask questions, the old questions for which he no longer has answers. Paulin's lonely Unionist begins the search for his own people. In other words, for home. In *Milkman*, Anna Burns describes a young woman whose habits and opinions make her a foreigner in her own community. Middle sister is an object of suspicion, the odd one out. Like Paulin's Unionist, she finds that home is not where it is supposed to be. And in Heaney's poem 'The Disappearing Island', settlers build a home which vanishes beneath their feet. Again, certainty melts away. Again, home is revealed to be a delusion.

These are hard lessons. Earlier generations of northern writers could construct new homes when they found reality wanting. C. S. Lewis populated the beloved landscapes of his birthplace with creatures of his own choosing. Forrest Reid did much the same thing, though with rather different motivations. But the writers who lived through the Troubles could not retreat into fantasy. To write well about their time and place, Heaney, Longley, and Mahon had to address the anxieties about home and belonging that have been a part of northern life since the plantation. This was not always done explicitly, of course. The homesick quality I associate with Northern Irish writing is, more often than not, a dark and silent undertow: the casual visitor who stumbles across a scene of horrifying, competing life in Mahon's 'A Disused Shed in Co. Wexford', the chattering corpse in Heaney's 'Bog Queen'. Both are macabre, uncanny images that a German might call *unheimlich*—literally, 'unhomelike'.

For the past fifty years, northern writing has been preoccupied with the grim realities of life in a divided society. This depiction of a culture in which so many feel displaced has been one of the vital contributions made by writers from Northern Ireland. But this has never been the sole focus. If a sense of homelessness and dislocation forms one pillar of northern writing, then the natural world forms the other. Indeed fields, trees, and birds have often supplied the language through which writers can express darker truths.

'The Blackbird of Belfast Lough' was written in Irish over a thousand years ago. It is a tiny poem about something that can still be seen today. A blackbird sits on a loughshore whin bush. The whin is in flower—massing blooms that, from a distance, resemble a yellow cloud. The blackbird sings. Seamus Heaney translated the poem like this:

The small bird
chirp-chirruped:
yellow neb,
a note-spurt.

Blackbird over
Lagan water,
clumps of yellow
whin-burst!

No one knows the identity of the original poet, though there has been speculation that he was a monk at Bangor Abbey, on the southern shore of the water-way now known as Belfast Lough. No matter. The blackbird has been trilling through northern writing for centuries.

Patrick Kavanagh addressed the blackbird as a fellow writer: 'O pagan poet, you / And I are one / In this—we lose our god / At set of sun' ('To a Blackbird', 1936). Derek Mahon wrote his own version of 'The Blackbird of Belfast Lough', taking the medieval verse into his own life: 'One morning in the month of June / I was coming out of this door...'

> *When from a bramble bush a hidden*
> *Blackbird suddenly gave tongue,*
> *Its diffident, resilient song*
> *Breaking the silence of the seas.*
>   —'A Blackbird' (1979)

William Carleton remembered a particular blackbird from his childhood: 'With the music of this bird I was so intensely delighted, that I used to go to bed every fine evening two hours before my usual time, for the express purpose of listening to the music. There was a back window in the bedroom where I slept; this I opened, and there I lay until I fell asleep with the melody in my ears.' And when he wrote an elegy for his brother, Heaney chose the blackbird as both proof of life and harbinger of death: 'On the grass when I arrive, / In the ivy when I leave' ('The Blackbird of Glanmore', 2006).

For Carleton and Heaney, the bird is a memory of home. Carleton recalls the beautiful glen that ran up behind his house. A summer evening, the open window. Heaney thinks back to his brother: 'Haunterson, lost brother—/ Cavorting through the yard, / So glad to see me home, / My homesick first term over.'

A memory of home. Everything that has been written in Northern Ireland—the thousands of poems, the hundreds of novels, the plays and songs and histories—everything comes down to this. Lewis, Reid, and MacNeice in their haunted houses. Kavanagh in Dublin, dreaming of the small farm he never should have left. Heaney digging up Mossbawn's forked root. The Ulster Unionist who turns away from the Strangers' House and runs through the streets of a foreign city, a city that was meant to be his birthright.

All that remains is memory of the lost home. Perhaps the blackbird's song offers hope that return is possible. That the homesick term will end at last.

Acknowledgements

I would like to thank Sean Desmond, my editor at Twelve, for his enormous patience and thoughtful critiques. Thanks also to my agent, William LoTurco, and to Sam Kashner, who gave me the courage to write this book. I am deeply grateful to Maurice Leitch for answering my questions about his work, and for telling me more about Ian Cochrane. Research for *The Strangers' House* was carried out in the McClay Library at Queen's University Belfast, and I am very appreciative of the help provided to me by the library staff, particularly those in Special Collections. Friends in Belfast deserve special thanks, especially Robert Crone and the late Douglas Carson. This book is dedicated to my parents, Trevor and Fiona—thank you.

Selected Bibliography

Bardon, Jonathan. *A History of Ulster.* 1992. Revised
Edition: Blackstaff Press, 2001.

Bartlett, Thomas. *Ireland: A History.* Cambridge University Press, 2010.

Carleton, William. *The Autobiography of William Carleton.*
1896. Revised Edition: MacGibbon & Kee, 1968.

Cochrane, Ian. *F for Ferg.* Victor Gollancz, 1980.

—. *Gone in the Head.* Routledge, 1974.

—. *A Streak of Madness.* Allen Lane, 1973.

Enniss, Stephen. *After the Titanic: A Life of Derek
Mahon.* Gill & Macmillan, 2014.

Forster, E. M. *Selected Letters of E. M. Forster.* Edited
by Mary Lago and P. N. Furbank. 2 Vols. Collins, 1983.

Haughton, Hugh. *The Poetry of Derek Mahon.* Oxford
University Press, 2007.

Heaney, Seamus. *District and Circle*. Faber and Faber, 2006.

—. *Finders Keepers: Selected Prose 1971–2001*. Faber and Faber, 2002.

—. *The Haw Lantern*. Faber and Faber, 1987.

—. *North*. Faber and Faber, 1975.

—. *Opened Ground: Poems 1966–1996*. Faber and Faber, 1998.

—. *Station Island*. Faber and Faber, 1984.

Kavanagh, Patrick. *Collected Poems*. Edited by Antoinette Quinn. Penguin, 2005.

—. *Collected Pruse*. Martin Brian & O'Keefe, 1973.

—. *Tarry Flynn*. Martin Brian & O'Keefe, 1972.

Kavanagh, Peter. *Sacred Keeper: A Biography of Patrick Kavanagh*. Goldsmith Press, 1979.

Lewis, C. S. *All My Road Before Me: The Diaries of C. S. Lewis*. Edited by Walter Hooper. HarperCollins, 1991.

—. *C. S. Lewis: Collected Letters Vols. I–III*. Edited by Walter Hooper. HarperCollins, 2000–2006.

—. *Surprised By Joy: The Shape of My Early Life*. Geoffrey Bles, 1955.

—. *They Stand Together: The Letters of C. S. Lewis to Arthur Greeves (1914–1963)*. Edited by Walter Hooper. Macmillan, 1979.

Longley, Edna. *Poetry in the Wars*. Bloodaxe Books, 1986.

Longley, Michael. *Collected Poems*. Cape Poetry, 2007.

—. *Sidelines: Selected Prose 1962–2015*. Enitharmon Press, 2017.

MacNeice, Louis. *Autumn Journal*. Faber and Faber, 1939.

—. *Collected Poems*. Edited by E. R. Dodds. Faber and Faber, 1966.

—. *Collected Poems*. Edited by Peter McDonald. Faber and Faber, 2007.

—. *Letters of Louis MacNeice*. Edited by Jonathan Allison. Faber and Faber, 2010.

—. *The Poetry of W. B. Yeats*. Faber and Faber, 1967.

—. *The Strings are False: An Unfinished Autobiography*. Faber and Faber, 1965.

Mahon, Derek. *Journalism: Selected Prose 1970–1995*. Edited by Terence Brown. Gallery Books, 1996.

—. *New Collected Poems*. Gallery Books, 2011.

McGuckian, Medbh. *The Unfixed Horizon: New Selected Poems*. Wake Forest University Press, 2015.

McKittrick, David, and David McVea. *Making Sense of the Troubles: A History of the Northern Ireland Conflict*. 2001. Revised Edition: Viking, 2012.

Muldoon, Paul. *Meeting the British*. Faber and Faber, 1987.

O'Driscoll, Dennis. *Stepping Stones: Interviews with Seamus Heaney.* Faber and Faber, 2008.

Parr, Connal. *Inventing the Myth: Political Passions and the Ulster Protestant Imagination.* Oxford University Press, 2017.

Quinn, Antoinette. *Patrick Kavanagh: A Biography.* Gill & Macmillan, 2001.

Reid, Forrest. *Apostate.* 1926. Reprint: Faber and Faber, 2011.

—. *Brian Westby.* 1934. Revised Edition: Valancourt Books, 2013.

—. *The Garden God.* 1905. Revised Edition: Valancourt Books, 2007.

—. *Private Road.* 1940. Reprint: Faber and Faber, 2011.

—. *The Tom Barber Trilogy.* Edited by Michael Matthew Kaylor. 2 Vols. Valancourt Books, 2011.

Stallworthy, Jon. *Louis MacNeice.* Faber and Faber, 1995.

Walker, Tom. *Louis MacNeice and the Irish Poetry of his Time.* Oxford University Press, 2015.

Wilson, A. N. *C. S. Lewis: A Biography.* William Collins, 1990.

Notes

Introduction

I don't think for a split second: Interview with Michael Longley, *The Honest Ulsterman* 78 (Summer 1985), reprinted in Michael Longley, *Sidelines: Selected Prose 1962–2015* (Enitharmon Press, 2017), p. 372.

When Seamus Heaney was asked about identity, he would answer with great care: See, for example, the interview with SH in Mark Carruthers, *Alternative Ulsters: Who Do We Think We Are?* (Liberties Press, 2014), pp. 135, 140–141.

Heaney described the poem: Dennis O'Driscoll, *Stepping Stones: Interviews with Seamus Heaney* (Faber and Faber, 2008), p. 287.

CHAPTER 1: *A product of long corridors*

My bad dreams: C. S. Lewis, *Surprised by Joy: The Shape of My Early Life* (Geoffrey Bles, 1955), p. 15.

His enduring dislike of Louis MacNeice: A. N. Wilson, *C. S. Lewis: A Biography* (William Collins, 1990), p. 99. Cautious attempts have been made to rehabilitate Lewis's poetry; see, for example, Malcolm Guite, 'Poet', in *The Cambridge Companion to C. S. Lewis*, eds. Robert MacSwain and Michael Ward (Cambridge University Press, 2010), pp. 294–310.

The drains did not drain: Lewis, *Surprised by Joy*, p. 17.

The New House is almost: Ibid., p. 17.

The chivalric adventures: Ibid., p. 20.

The operation to save Flora: George Sayer, *Jack: C. S. Lewis and His Times* (MacMillan, 1988), p. 22.

Like all Irish people: Letter from C. S. Lewis to Arthur Greeves, 27 May 1917, in *C. S. Lewis: Collected Letters, Volume 1*, ed. Walter Hooper (HarperCollins, 2000), p. 310.

'Tis true that: Letter from C. S. Lewis to Arthur Greeves, 24 July 1917, ibid., p. 330.

The Mac Canns, so far as they professed a religion: James Stephens, *The Demi-Gods* (MacMillan, 1914), p. 18.

The religious, political and social cleavage: Quoted in Sayer, *Jack*, pp. 32–33.

The daemonic character: Quote from *Introduction* by C. S. Lewis, written in 1950, in *C. S. Lewis: Narrative Poems*, ed. Walter Hooper (Geoffrey Bles, 1969), p. 4.

Certainly the actual country: Letter from C. S. Lewis to Warren Lewis, 13 April 1929, in Hooper, *Letters, Vol. 1*, p. 792.

Great adventure: Letter from C. S. Lewis to Albert Lewis, 25 October 1921, ibid., p. 587.

Your news of a post: Letter from C. S. Lewis to Albert Lewis, 18 May 1922, ibid., p. 590.

I keep on hearing: Letter from C. S. Lewis to Albert Lewis, 31 August 1921, ibid., p. 586.

Iron Curtain: Letter from C. S. Lewis to Vera Gebbert, 28 July 1952, in *C. S. Lewis: Collected Letters, Volume 3*, ed. Walter Hooper (HarperCollins, 2009), p. 219.

I should have thought that a pack of British boys: William Golding, *Lord of the Flies* (Faber and Faber, 1954), p. 224.

Not exciting: Letter from C. S. Lewis to Arthur Greeves, 27 May 1917, in Hooper, *Letters, Vol. 1*, p. 310.

Cornwall seemed an imitation of Antrim: Letter from C. S. Lewis to Warren Lewis, 7 August 1921, ibid., p. 580.

I often think how lovely: Letter from C. S. Lewis to Arthur Greeves, 6 June 1917, ibid., p. 313.

I have seen landscapes: C. S. Lewis, 'On Stories', *Of This and Other Worlds* (Collins, 1982), p. 31.

That part of Rostrevor: 'If you didn't find Narnia in your own wardrobe...' The *Observer*, 4 December 2005; see also the official

tourism website for Northern Ireland: https://discovernorth
ernireland.com/things-to-do/the-narnia-trail-p722461.

These words have been attributed to Lewis on many occa-
sions. Although often cited as a quote from a letter to Warren
Lewis, I have failed to find the original source in C. S. Lewis's
published correspondence. On balance I believe the quote to be
genuine, not least because Lewis had a particular attachment to
Carlingford Lough and the surrounding areas—the Mournes to
the north, and the Cooley Peninsula to the south. Rostrevor sits
at the heart of this region. The letter may well await publication in Oxford's Bodleian Library, the Marion E. Wade Center
at Wheaton College, or a private collection.

I think the only thing for you to do: Letter from C. S. Lewis to
Arthur Greeves, 18 August 1930, in Hooper, *Letters, Vol. 1*,
p. 927.

Your particular taste: Letter from C. S. Lewis to Arthur Greeves,
6 March 1917, in *They Stand Together: The Letters of C. S. Lewis to
Arthur Greeves 1914–1963*, ed. Walter Hooper (MacMillan, 1979),
p. 173.

Be careful of Reid: Letter from C. S. Lewis to Arthur Greeves, 8
November 1931, ibid., p. 430.

CHAPTER 2: *Be careful of Reid*

Just then, when his lips: Forrest Reid, *The Garden God: A Tale of Two
Boys* (1905; repr., Valancourt Books, 2007), p. 28.

The messenger of Eros: Ibid., p. 13.

During the American Civil War: Forrest Reid, *Apostate* (1926;
repr., Faber and Faber, 2011), p. 12.

What I saw there: Ibid., p. 9.

Divine homesickness: Ibid., p. 7.

Reid recalled: Ibid., p. 26.

Like a vast rotting body: Ibid., p. 40.

How often had I: Ibid., p. 42.

And presently, out from the leafy shadow: Ibid., p. 60.

Every fault except insincerity: Ibid., p. 145.

Hush! Speak lower: Reid, *The Garden God*, p. 27.

You are too young for an athlete: Ibid., p. 59.

That thing which may be best: Ibid., p. 60.

To the darkest corner: Brian Taylor, *The Green Avenue: The Life and Writings of Forrest Reid, 1875–1947* (Cambridge University Press, 1980), p. 47.

Attempted to kill himself: Reid, *Apostate*, pp. 164–5.

An opiate beauty: Ibid., p. 26.

And the Master was not pleased: Forrest Reid, *Private Road* (1940; repr., Faber and Faber, 2011), p. 65.

Strange moral timidity: Ibid., p. 70.

Described him as a homosexual: Stephen Gilbert, 'A Successful Man', *Threshold* 28 (Spring 1977), p. 108.

Of actual homosexual goings-on: Ibid., p. 108.

I have written a novel which cannot be published: Letter from E. M. Forster to Forrest Reid, 23 January 1915, in *Selected Letters of E. M. Forster, Vol. 1*, eds. Mary Lago and P. N. Furbank (Collins, 1983), p. 139.

I have heard you feel things: Ibid., p. 139.

Sometimes, indeed, the sunshine: Reid, *Apostate*, p. 174.

He recalled the way: Ibid., p. 176.

During all the nineteen years I knew him: Gilbert, 'A Successful Man', p. 106.

He was very untidy: Forrest Reid, *Brian Westby* (1934; repr., Valancourt Books, 2013), p. 18.

Winter coyly hiding: John McGahern, 'Brian Westby', *Threshold* 28 (Spring 1977), p. 45.

This was not the psychology: Reid, *Brian Westby*, p. 154.

You can see the author knew this: Ibid., pp. 17–18.

Jamesian lamps: McGahern, 'Brian Westby', p. 43.

The rain had thickened: Reid, *Brian Westby*, p. 64.

All that he valued was learnt here: E. M. Forster, 'Forrest Reid Memorial Address: October 10th, 1952', *Threshold* 28 (Spring 1977), p. 4.

One slides up to it at dawn: E. M. Forster, 'Forrest Reid', *Abinger Harvest* (Edward Arnold, 1936), p. 92.

He found the place: Reid, *Brian Westby*, p. 206.

During air raids: Taylor, *The Green Avenue*, p. 166.

Some very queer friends: Forrest Reid, *Uncle Stephen, The Tom Barber Trilogy, Vol. 1* (Valancourt Books, 2011), p. 15.

Have made a lovely magician: Ibid., p. 125.

All the characters have: Forster, 'Forrest Reid', p. 95.

It is striking how convinced: Connal Parr, *Inventing the Myth: Political Passions and the Ulster Protestant Imagination* (Oxford University Press, 2017), p. 7.

Although Irish: Reid, *Private Road*, p. 35.

The boy looked at him: Reid, *Brian Westby*, pp. 15–16.

CHAPTER 3: *Grey Crow & the lawyer*

I beheld my first celebrity: Reid, *Apostate*, p. 46.

His very name became a slur: Alan Sinfield, ' "I See It Is My *Name* That Terrifies": Wilde in the Twentieth Century', in *The Wilde Legacy*, ed. Eiléan Ní Chuilleanáin (Four Courts Press, 2003), p. 137.

Everything that tends to sordidness: Letter from C. S. Lewis to Arthur Greeves, 6 March 1917, in Hooper, *They Stand Together*, p. 173.

An unspeakable of the Oscar Wilde sort: E. M. Forster, *Maurice*, ed. Philip Gardner (Andre Deutsch, 1999), p. 134.

Oscar Wilde was not an Irishman: Myles na Gopaleen, the *Irish Times*, 11 September 1954, quoted in Éibhear Walshe, *Oscar's Shadow: Wilde, Homosexuality and Modern Ireland* (Cork University Press, 2011), p. 48.

Frustration at having to explain: Jerusha McCormack, 'Preface', in *Wilde the Irishman*, ed. Jerusha McCormack (Yale University Press, 1998), p. xv.

Grey Crow: Richard Ellmann, *Oscar Wilde* (Hamish Hamilton, 1987), p. 21.

English history was the only history: Owen Dudley Edwards, 'Impressions of an Irish Sphinx', McCormack, *Wilde the Irishman*, pp. 63–64.

His name was removed: Ellmann, *Oscar Wilde*, p. 25.

CHAPTER 4: *Genius but no education*

Fortunately for Patrick: Peter Kavanagh, *Sacred Keeper: A Biography of Patrick Kavanagh* (Goldsmith Press, 1979), p. 24.

When they came to the conflict: William Carleton, *The Autobiography of William Carleton* (1896; rev. ed., MacGibbon & Kee, 1968), p. 36.

I wanted a fight: Patrick Kavanagh, *The Green Fool* (1938; Penguin Classics, 2001), p. 129.

What had happened was this: Ibid., pp. 134–135.

What kind of a paper is this?: Ibid., p. 193.

A true national culture: Letter from George Russell to W. B. Yeats, 10 March 1921, in *Letters to W. B. Yeats, Vol. II*, eds. Richard J. Finneran, George Mills Harper, and William M. Murphy (MacMillan Press, 1977), p. 374.

The tramp–necessary rectangular knee patches: Kavanagh, *The Green Fool*, p. 222.

Yer not a tramp: Ibid., pp. 226–227.

He appeared quite certain: Ibid., p. 228.

Opened the door to me: Ibid., p. 228.

There is plenty of talent in Ireland today: Letter from George Russell to W. B. Yeats, April 1932, in Finneran, Harper, and Murphy, *Letters to W. B. Yeats, Vol. II*, p. 533.

If you let it burn: W. B. Yeats, *The Celtic Twilight* (1893, 1902; new ed., Colin Smythe, 1981), p. 109.

To the wise peasant: Ibid., p. 108.

One night as I sat eating: Ibid., p. 109.

Batting the river with its hands: Ibid., p. 35.

The visionary melancholy: Ibid., p. 34.

I feel alien to everything except the earth itself: Letter from George Russell to W. B. Yeats, 5 April 1932, in Finneran, Harper, and Murphy, *Letters to W. B. Yeats, Vol. II*, p. 532.

Like a lout I knew in boyhood: Letter from George Russell to W. B. Yeats, 6 March 1932, ibid., p. 531.

The Irish Academy of Letters meets: Letter from Louis MacNeice to Eleanor Clark, 16 July 1939, in *Letters of Louis MacNeice*, ed. Jonathan Allison (Faber and Faber, 2010), p. 351.

I have hopes that we may have a new young genius: Letter from George Russell to W. B. Yeats, 17 December 1932, in Finneran, Harper, and Murphy, *Letters to W. B. Yeats, Vol. II*, pp. 547–548.

CHAPTER 5: *The lamp was dark beside my bed*

These metres dictated: J. E. Caerwyn Williams and Patrick K. Ford, *The Irish Literary Tradition* (University of Wales Press, 1992), p. 156.

What in English: James Carney, *Medieval Irish Lyrics & The Irish Bardic Poet* (Dolmen Press, 1985), p. xi.

The said subject having been given: Osborn Bergin, *Irish Bardic Poetry*, eds. David Greene and Fergus Kelly (Dublin Institute for Advanced Studies, 1970), p. 6.

Must have owed its origin: Williams and Ford, *The Irish Literary Tradition*, p. 162.

In poetry to the English: Ibid., p. 171.

Without secrecy and darkness: Bergin, *Irish Bardic Poetry*, p. 265.

Free verse on the open road: Ibid., p. 270.

The family was ostracised by the community at first: Jon Stallworthy, *Louis MacNeice* (Faber and Faber, 1995), p. 21.

Things project other things: Louis MacNeice, *The Strings are False* (Faber and Faber, 1965), p. 38.

And Annie the cook had a riddle: Ibid., p. 38.

There was a kind of a noise: Ibid., p. 46.

Thinghood: Louis MacNeice, *The Poetry of W. B. Yeats* (Faber, 1967), p. 15.

Thanks awfully for introducing me to Art: Letter from Louis MacNeice to Anthony Blunt, 26 September 1926, in Allison, *Letters*, p. 124.

The family is just like: Letter from Louis MacNeice to Anthony Blunt, 31 December 1927, ibid., pp. 180–181.

Have just read such a bad novel: Letter from Louis MacNeice to Anthony Blunt, 15 February 1928, ibid., p. 184. The novel young Louis disliked so much was presumably *The Sun Also Rises* (1926).

Stuck once more among: Letter from Louis MacNeice to Anthony Blunt, 29 February 1928, ibid., p. 185.

Marxism never held much allure: Stallworthy, *Louis MacNeice*, p. 180.

As Edna Longley has observed: Edna Longley, *Poetry in the Wars* (Bloodaxe Books, 1986), p. 90.

It was Dodds who brought the two men together: E. R. Dodds, *Missing Persons: An Autobiography* (Oxford, 1977), p. 122.

7 Middagh Street: Stallworthy, *Louis MacNeice*, pp. 284–285.

I recognized the long dark head: John Hewitt, *A North Light: Twenty-Five Years in a Municipal Art Gallery*, eds. Frank Ferguson and Kathryn White (Four Courts Press, 2013), p. 185.

Bent black safety pin of the eyes: Bob Pocock, 'Louis MacNeice, a Radio Portrait' (7 September 1966), quoted in Stallworthy, *Louis MacNeice*, p. 349.

Absolutely silent and astonishingly ugly: Walter Hooper, ed., *All My Road Before Me: The Diaries of C. S. Lewis, 1922–1927* (HarperCollins, 1991), p. 437.

Leaning back against the chimney piece: Stephen Spender, *The Thirties and After: Poetry, Politics, People, 1933–75* (Fontana, 1978), p. 233.

Did MacNeice come from the Northern coast: Stephen Spender, 'The Brilliant Mr. MacNeice', *New Republic*, 28 January 1967.

It was a bit disappointing, actually: Maurice Leitch, interview with the author, London, 6 June 2019.

I saw Louis standing: Spender, *The Thirties*, p. 265.

An unfinished history of astrology: Dodds, *Missing Persons*, p. 188.

Meet the U.S. Army: Stallworthy, *Louis MacNeice*, pp. 318–319.

Go-as-you-please affair: I. A. Williams, 'Mr. MacNeice at the Zoo', the *Times Literary Supplement*, 12 November 1938.

The English school system: Derek Mahon, 'MacNeice in Ireland and England', in *Journalism: Selected Prose 1970–1995*, ed. Terence Brown (Gallery Press, 1996), p. 21.

His poetry is of largely English derivation: Ibid., pp. 21–22.

For them the rhythm of their race: 'Tendencies in Modern Poetry: A Discussion between Prof. F. R. Higgins and Louis MacNeice', *The Listener*, 27 July 1939 (Vol. XXII, No. 550), p. 185.

American Victorian: Ibid., p. 185.

For him poetry is merely: Ibid., p. 185.

I don't believe that a poet born: Ibid., p. 186.

On those premises: Ibid., p. 185.

In some respects: Ibid., p. 185.

The man I had the radio discussion with: Letter from Louis MacNeice to Eleanor Clark, 16 July 1939, in Allison, *Letters*, pp. 350–351.

Irish parentage: Letter from Louis MacNeice to Ellen Borden Stevenson, 21 March 1953, ibid., p. 562.

Reminded a concerned T. S. Eliot: Letter from Louis MacNeice to T. S. Eliot, 14 September 1939, ibid., p. 355.

Never prepared to enslave: Dodds, *Missing Persons*, p. 118.

Even now many Englishmen: MacNeice, *Poetry of W. B. Yeats*, p. 52.

A stratum: Letter from Louis MacNeice to Eleanor Clark, 21 May 1940, in Allison, *Letters*, p. 395.

It is about time someone: Letter from Louis MacNeice to Anthony Blunt, 19 November 1935, ibid., p. 259.

Ireland is the Malvolio of the nations: George Bernard Shaw, 'How to Settle the Irish Question', in *The Matter with Ireland*, eds. David H. Greene and Dan H. Laurence (Rupert Hart-Davis, 1962), p. 145.

Drenched in a rainstorm: Stallworthy, *Louis MacNeice*, p. 475.

CHAPTER 6: *Forked root*

MASKED CONTRACTORS—ATTACK LOYALISM AT YOUR OWN RISK: 'Police Working to Get Sinister Avoniel Bonfire Graffiti Removed at "Earliest Opportunity"', *Belfast Telegraph*, 14 July 2019.

Much more *thrilling*: Letter from Philip Larkin to Monica Jones, 12 July 1951, in *Letters to Monica*, ed. Anthony Thwaite (Faber and Faber, 2010), p. 49.

Inhuman and degrading: David McKittrick and David McVea, *Making Sense of the Troubles: A History of the Northern Ireland Conflict* (2000; rev. ed., Viking, 2012), p. 78.

More than once: Jake O'Kane, 'Nationalists Burned Bonfires Too—but We Were Only Kids Back Then', the *Irish News*, 13 July 2019.

Fire was what I loved: Seamus Deane, *Reading in the Dark* (1996; Vintage, 2019), p. 33.

A conscious attempt to offer an alternative: Parr, *Inventing the Myth*, pp. 26–27.

A deeply political event: 'Féile an Phobail: Calls for Police Investigation after Pro-IRA Chanting', *Belfast Telegraph*, 13 August 2019; 'Young Children among Those Chanting IRA Support at Féile', the *Irish News*, 17 August 2021; 'Féile "Pro-IRA" Chanting Prompts Unionist Councillor to Call on Public Money to Be Withdrawn from Event', *Belfast Telegraph*, 16 August 2021.

A one-storey, longish: O'Driscoll, *Stepping Stones*, p. 3.

Big flubby snorts: Ibid., p. 15.

Omphalos: Seamus Heaney, 'Mossbawn', *Finders Keepers: Selected Prose, 1971–2001* (Faber and Faber, 2002), p. 3.

A subsistence-level life: O'Driscoll, *Stepping Stones*, p. 8.

The rattle of Orange drums: Heaney, 'Mossbawn', p. 6.

The planters came: Thomas Bartlett, *Ireland: A History* (Cambridge University Press, 2010), pp. 100–101.

Conor Roe Maguire: Jonathan Bardon, *The Plantation of Ulster* (Gill & MacMillan, 2011), p. 193.

Irish tenants often outnumbered: Bartlett, *Ireland*, p. 103.

The writer becomes earth-turner, archaeologist: On Heaney as poetic excavator, see, for example, *Poets from the North of Ireland*, ed. Frank Ormsby (Blackstaff Press, 1979), pp. 8–9.

Kavanagh walked into my ear: O'Driscoll, *Stepping Stones*, p. 192.

When, under the evil aegis: Patrick Kavanagh, 'Self Portrait', *Collected Pruse* (Martin Brian & O'Keefe, 1973), p. 13.

I am humble enough: Ibid., p. 13.

The things that really matter: Ibid., pp. 18–19.

There was the saying: Maurice Leitch, interview with the author, London, 6 June 2019.

In Ulster where you find the drumlins: E. Estyn Evans, *Ulster: The Common Ground* (Lilliput Press, 1984), p. 7.

Poetic and visionary: Ibid., p. 7.

We lived in a little house right out in the country: Quoted in Paul Magrath, 'Ian Cochrane: Obituary', the *Independent*, 18 September 2004.

In other countries: Ian Cochrane, *A Streak of Madness* (Allen Lane, 1973), p. 10.

This is my brother Bill: Ian Cochrane, *F for Ferg* (1980; repr., Turnpike Books, 2018), pp. 20–21.

A Norwegian fruit merchant: Ibid., p. 11.

There's something very real: Ibid., p. 9.

Sporting long flowing woollen scarves: Maurice Leitch, 'Ian Cochrane: Obituary', the *Guardian*, 23 September 2004.

It was a one-room flat: Maurice Leitch, interview with the author. London, 6 June 2019.

Combative and no-holds-barred: Interview with Michael Longley, *The Honest Ulsterman* 78 (Summer 1985), in Longley, *Sidelines*, p. 372.

The great triumvirate of Northern poets: R. F. Foster, *On Seamus Heaney* (Princeton University Press, 2020), p. 10.

The 1947 Education Act: Ormsby, *Poets*, p. 7.

All thanks to the system: O'Driscoll, *Stepping Stones*, p. 31.

Roughen up: Ibid., p. 40.

The minute I opened it: Ibid., p. 158.

CHAPTER 7: *Teethmarks*

A bomb exploded in the heart of Dublin: 'From the Archives: February 8th, 1971,' the *Irish Times*, 8 February 2012.

Wolfe's brother Matthew: Marianne Elliott, *Wolfe Tone* (1989; rev. ed., Liverpool University Press, 2012), p. 254.

Another brother, Arthur, fought for the United States: Ibid., p. 390.

His sister, Mary, spied for France: Thomas Bartlett, ed., *Life of Theobald Wolfe Tone* (Lilliput Press, 1998), p. vii.

With her standing and running rigging all cut to pieces: William James, *The Naval History of Great Britain, Vol. 2* (1827; repr., Macmillan, 1902), p. 145.

Last night it blew a perfect hurricane: Bartlett, *Life of Theobald Wolfe Tone*, p. 671.

There was food and drink: Anna Burns, *Milkman* (Faber and Faber, 2018), p. 25.

They could be up to anything in it: Ibid., p. 156.

One of those intemperate: Ibid., p. 199.

In it he'd threatened to kill himself: Ibid., p. 307.

And thus to repay: Letter from Anton Chekhov to A. S. Suvorin, 9 March 1890, in *Sakhalin Island*, Anton Chekhov, trans. Brian Reeve (1895; Alma Classics, 2019), p. 478.

Live, like the Irish: Ibid., p. 84.

Write, write, bloody write: Ibid., p. 73.

Self-accusation: O'Driscoll, *Stepping Stones*, p. 259.

If I had followed the logic: Ibid., p. 259.

The only thing they have in common: Quoted in Colm Tóibín, 'Introduction', *Black Robe* (1985; new ed., Apollo, 2017), p. ix.

Laforgue felt himself start: Brian Moore, *Black Robe* (1985; new ed., Apollo, 2017), p. 68.

A sorcerer: Ibid., pp. 69–70.

The poets from the South: Michaela Schrage-Früh, 'An Interview with Medbh McGuckian', *Contemporary Literature*, Vol. 46, No. 1 (Spring 2005), p. 9.

Floating in the trees: Ibid., p. 6.

Forrest Reid Memorial Prize: Stephen Enniss, *After the* Titanic*: A Life of Derek Mahon* (Gill & MacMillan, 2014), p. 24.

A brief two-line *memento-mori*: Hugh Haughton, *The Poetry of Derek Mahon* (Oxford University Press, 2007), p. 351.

Lapsed classicist: Interview with Michael Longley, *The Honest Ulsterman* 78 (Summer 1985), in Longley, *Sidelines*, p. 366.

Over-mythologised: 'A Jovial Hullabaloo,' Longley, *Sidelines*, p. 305.

The Shorland crew members offer no explanation: Chairman, Mr Justice Scarman, *Violence and Civil Disturbances in Northern Ireland in 1969: Report of Tribunal of Inquiry* (HMSO, 1972), p. 167.

CHAPTER 8: *The Strangers' House*

With the music of this bird: Carleton, *Autobiography*, p. 52.

Index

About the Author

Alexander Poots was born in London in 1985. After studying at the University of Manchester and Magdalen College, Oxford, he worked as a bookseller. *The Strangers' House* is his first book. He lives in Belfast.